THE LOBSTER STORE

Suzanne B. Page

authorHOUSE™

1663 LIBERTY DRIVE, SUITE 200
BLOOMINGTON, INDIANA 47403
(800) 839-8640
WWW.AUTHORHOUSE.COM

First published by AuthorHouse 09/01/05

ISBN: 1-4208-6557-9 (sc)

Library of Congress Control Number: 2005905453

Printed in the United States of America
Bloomington, Indiana

This book is printed on acid-free paper.

Acknowledgements

I want to thank my husband John for his devotion and efforts to produce the final copy of The LOBSTER STORE on our laptop computer. We decided to use his painting of Joan's cottage for the cover and then he contributed the chapter sketches. I could not have accomplished the project without his enduring interest and loving support.

FOREWORD

In the fall of 2003 Joan Beal sent me a set of cassette tapes on which she had recorded memorable stories from her life as a fisherman's daughter. Throughout a very cold, snowy Vermont winter and short spring, I sat in our sunny bay window transcribing her words into my notebook. In June, however, the work stopped as I was operated on for ovarian cancer. The cancer had spread so more surgery was necessary and I couldn't begin the prescribed chemotherapy until September. My extreme weakness almost brought the writing to a halt. By January the loving prayers of my friends and family gave me inspiration and strength. I consider the writing of this book a very real contribution to my recovery.

CHAPTER ONE

"Mmmmmmm", "mmmmmmmm", "mmmmmmmmmmmm", sounded the marine engines of Maine lobster boats that pre-dawn morning in June 2003. Daddy and I had each arisen, still tired from the short summer night, at 4 AM to begin the day checking our 300 traps and hauling the treasured lobsters. After pulling on his fishing clothes, he always ate his simple breakfast of 3 slices of Mama's homemade bread toasted and spread with her strawberry jam all washed down with hot tea. Before leaving the kitchen he would pick up the crab meat sandwiches and thermoses of tea Mama had prepared for our lunch. He would carry them to his truck and drive down to our wharf where the dinghy was moored. In my house, overlooking the wharf, I heard him drive past, my signal for stepping out my door and walking down the rocky hillside to join him. Before leaving my kitchen, I filled my crock pot with meat and vegetables so there would be a good meal waiting for me at the end of the long hard day. I am 53 now and have been my father's "sternman" on the <u>Marion P</u>, the most beautiful boat in the cove, for 41 years.

As we placed ourselves and our gear in the little dinghy, I began to think about the routine we had followed faithfully for so long. Daddy really was proud of his boat, of his work, of me, and the store of memories we shared.Because he was so handsome and so kind to me, I wanted to be with him all the time. When I was too little to go out with him, my joy came at his daily return. Mama would be getting supper. After removing his boots by the front door, Daddy always went into the kitchen to wash up. On his way he would stop to let me sit down on his feet for a ride. In hesitant steps he shuffled out to the kitchen, holding my hands tightly and smiling down at me; I could never get enough time with him. And so, as I grew up watching his daily activities and listening to him tell Mama about the size of the lobsters, the number of crabs he had brought her and the other fishing stories, I knew that someday I would be an important part of that life.

Before Daddy could actually use me as a helper on the boat, he and Mama gave me many jobs that stimulated me to be helpful. He taught me how to knit the bait bags. He made it look so easy because his 4 x 6 mesh bags always turned out perfect. Mine were so loose that at first the bait just floated through the mesh, out through the trap slots into the beaks of the waiting hungry gulls. Always hovering nearby, when they saw the clumsily knit larger bag of bait being put in the trap, they knew a meal was forthcoming!

After inspecting and accepting my first bags, Daddy declared that my hard work had earned me a ride on the boat, only a ride. My big job was to stay out of his and his helper's way. I loved watching each trap as he winched it up, opened it and reached in to pull out the contents. Sometimes there would be 2 or 3 lobsters, a few crabs and maybe a sculpin. Daddy would measure the lobsters and either pass them back for banding or, if too short, toss them back to sea. The helper would take out the crabs to save them for Mama and then remove the old bait bag and replace it with a full one. The whole process fascinated and thrilled me. I loved the smell of the ocean and the sound of the winch working to haul up the trap. I loved the way the gulls screeched as they flapped around our boat, like a watchful air guard for an important government ship at sea. Most of all, I loved watching my daddy in his rubber apron and boots hauling in the product that provided us with the best life I could ever imagine.

Early that same morning my older brother, Johnny, was also up and ready for his day's work hauling a refrigerated truck load of shellfish down to New York City or New Jersey. He loves driving as much now as he did when he was a boy and Daddy would let him climb up on the grader or the snow plow to steer. Johnny's interest in moving vehicles led him into the job that allows him to nurture his independence while providing sustenance for his bachelor life.

As a family we have lived at and loved Black Duck Cove on Great Wass Island all of our lives. The isolation of our early years was enhanced by the encouragement Mama and Daddy gave us to develop imaginative play while learning about our environment and Daddy's work. Johnny and I scampered up and down the rocky shores developing strong legs while learning about tidal pools and razorfish.. Although we wanted to help with everything related to lobster fishing we usually had more interest in imitating the real process or breaking away on adventures of our own in the shore hugging woods. Daddy never scolded us for purloining his ropes and tools or using scraps he might have been saving for some maritime purpose. Instead, it seemed as if he didn't know or care that his materials were going into miniature rafts and tree houses.

Daddy's work ethic coupled with his integrity and sense of humor have made him a respected lobsterman all his life. His great grandfather, Barney Beal, chose his island, the access to Great Wass, for his home. His house, the oldest on the island, stands today flanked by seaside cottages of other island folk. In fact, this same Barney

Beal has a thriving restaurant named for him. Daddy never really planned to do anything else and has been successful with his choice. He did the daily hard work, which has taken its toll on his body; however his spirit is as lively as ever. No challenge is too great, no sea is too overpowering for his skill as the skipper of his boat. He is meticulous in his care of the <u>Marion P</u> knowing that she will always respond to his needs in rough seas or calm. On the daily run from one trap to another along lines he established years ago he maneuvers his craft with skill and precision. He knows the rocks and shoals and how they are in relation to the tides. The tidal schedule, always a mystery to newcomers on the islands or tourists, is as familiar to him as a railroad schedule is to daily commuters. Sometimes we take passengers on a regular hauling day whose wide eyes and open mouths express their awe of Daddy as the master of his boat. I am so proud of what he has accomplished in life and know that Mama is glad that she accepted his proposal so many years ago.

They had actually met in high school. She saw him at a social function and was attracted immediately. When he left to go into the Navy, Mama helped his grandfather with letters to and from Elmer. She would write the ones from Maine and then read Elmer's to his grandfather aloud. One time she read "My girl has dropped me." Mama's heart fluttered remembering how he had put his hands on her waist to move her away from the punch bowl at that high school party where they met. She decided right then that he would be the one for her. They married, added Johnny and then me to the family.

When I was two years old we rented an Alpine cottage on Beals Island for the winter and spring. Daddy's boat was being repaired so he went fishing with his brother, Uncle Esten.

I remember one winter day he came home with frost on his cap, coat, mittens and eyelashes. His face was as ruddy as one of the winter apples Mama had on the table. He took off his outer wear and picked me up.

"Not much fishing today. It was so cold out there. I had to wade waist deep through the snow to get to the boat. It was froze in; had to dig it out!"

"Why didn't you come home, Daddy?"

"Well, darlin', your daddy has to earn some money to pay the rent on this cottage, buy food for us to eat and pay for repairs on my own boat. The Lord has blessed me with this work, helpin' your uncle Esten. If we can haul some every day, we can make it."

And so the winter passed: short, dark, cold days with Daddy at sea and Mama at the stove making good food to keep us all well fed.

Finally spring came with longer days and Daddy's chance to work on the cottage in the late afternoon. It needed roof repair so he set up a stagin' to help him safely work on that steeply slanting surface. I loved watching him crawl around up there like a monkey.

One late afternoon while Mama was in the kitchen cooking supper, I decided I could get up there by my Daddy. Only two and a half years old, somehow I climbed up!

Daddy yelled, "Marion, Marion, come out here now. This baby has climbed up to the roof!"

I just sat there, perched in a dormer, smiling down at Mama.

"Now you just stay right there 'til I can help you," Mama ordered.

Not wanting to climb up there herself, she actually talked me down. She was scared to death and kept moving around to be directly beneath where I was crawling backwards to catch me if I fell. I didn't. Mama didn't know whether to scold me or hug me she was so relieved to have me on solid ground.

Soon after that on a warm spring afternoon I decided to take my doll for a walk. It made me feel all grown up to get her ready, tuck her down in the carriage and then set out for a stroll right in the street. Well, I hadn't gone very far when a car pulled up behind me. A boy named Leonard had to slam on his brakes and shear the car to avoid hitting me. He was some upset, probably more scared than angry. He jumped out of the car, ran to the yard and broke a little alder switch off the bush by the door. Wide-eyed, I just stood there waiting for him to use the switch on me. He did, very lightly, saying "Don't you ever get in the road again." Then he marched to the door dragging me along.

Mama answered his knock and said, "Why, what's happened here?"

"Well, Ma'am, your little girl was pushin' her carriage right out there, in the middle of the road. Now, I just gave her a little switchin' and told her to stay out of the road."

Mama thanked him, took my hand and pulled me into the house. She jawed me good but that didn't scare me as much as Leonard did. I was afraid of Leonard from then on, even into my teen years.

Later in the summer we moved back to our home at Black Duck Cove on Great Wass Island. We are all still there, I in their remodeled first home, they in their new house and Johnny in a cottage. Daddy was so happy to have his boat ready to work again.

In late winter of that year one day Mama and Daddy went out "birding." It was a wonderful way to supplement our basic diet of seafood. They were so glad the season was still open for Sea Ducks, Black Ducks and Whistlers. At that time there was no limit on birds so they stayed out until they had twenty-five or thirty to bring home. Because Della and Richard (our adopted grandparents) were living with us that winter, they watched us when Mama and Daddy were out. Della would also have a good supper ready when they returned.

On this particular day in late January, they did not return until almost dark. We all were worried. Finally we heard noises in the yard and saw Daddy slowly approaching carrying Mama in his arms. I ran out looking in wonder at the unusual scene before me. "Daddy, what's the matter with Mama?"

"Well, darlin', I think your Mama broke her leg. We had about all the birds we could carry and had just started home when she slipped on the ice out there on Big Pond. Well sir, we were about three and a half miles from home, so I said, 'Marion dear, I'm going to have to carry you.'" Mama broke in with her reply: "I said, 'Why how can you do that? We've got these heavy guns and all the birds!'" Daddy said he told her, "Now just don't worry. I'll get you home as soon as I can. First let me splinter that leg to keep it straight." He broke off two nice witchwood branches, peeled them and then used her scarf to wrap them securely around her leg.

Then the work began! He carefully picked her up and began trudging through the snow until he was too tired to go another step. He gently put her down and said, "Now, Marion, you try to get comfortable here while I go back for the birds and our guns."

Mama said she huddled down determined not to think about the encroaching darkness but thankful that Daddy could follow the path he had heavily stomped in the snow. All she could do was wait, straining her eyes in the direction of his anxiously anticipated approach. Her heart warmed when she saw his ungainly figure in the distance, loaded down as he was, coming steadily towards her.

Daddy followed that scheme, carrying Mama, depositing her carefully in the snow and then going back for the baggage until he made it to our doorstep. After the short telling of this account, they rushed to get ready to take Mama to the doctor in Jonesport. At that time there was no bridge across Moosabec Reach to the mainland so Daddy took her on the ferry. Daddy had only five dollars in his pocket; the doctor accepted that as his fee for putting her leg in a cast. She wore it for six weeks.

When they got back home that night, Della and Richard had the big pails of boiling water ready and we all pitched in and helped. Richard dipped the birds in the boiling water, Della helped Mama cut off the heads with big knives, Daddy cleaned them and then Johnny and I got to help pick off the feathers. We saved them for Mama to fill pillows. The smell was awful but the rewards were great! The day after the shooting, Mama and Della jarred the birds which we feasted on at many meals well into spring.

That experience was hard on Mama because of trying to do everything on crutches. Except for helping pick feathers that night, I caused her even more problems.

The next day Johnny and I were outside playing. He had some very pretty little trucks that we liked to run all over the yard, in the snow, in the mud and on the bare patches of the driveway.

"Johnny, give me that red one."

"No, Titter, I want to take it in the mud."

"Johnny, give it to me! I want to play with it on the snow!"

I remember crying and feeling so angry at him that I just ran off into the woods to hide.

Johnny ran into the house, "Mama, Titter has run away!"

Poor Mama hobbled to the door and then out in the yard, scared to death that I might have fallen into the hand dug well only one hundred feet from the house. She called and called: "Titter, Titter; you come here right now!"

I was lying on my belly and had no desire to be found. Oh how she hollered! Suddenly we heard the rare frightening sound of a jet flying overhead. Mama yelled "Joanie, you come here right now or that airplane will get you!"

I jumped up and ran straight into her waiting arms. Johnny did the same. From then on we were both scared of airplanes. Mama scolded us both and really jawed me for running away. She said afterwards that she shouldn't have done that but it was the only thing she could think of at that time. She certainly couldn't hunt me down on crutches!

CHAPTER 2

Mama worked so hard all the time keeping the house, doing the laundry, cooking the meals and helping Daddy however she could. Her work days were so often interrupted by unplanned trips to a doctor in Jonesport or the hospital in Machias or, more often, to the kitchen dispensary. Because Johnny and I loved to play outside, like all children we were unaware of potential danger. We had our share of accidents.

One day Mama was down on the wharf painting the trap buoys. Johnny had started school so I had a new playmate, my Pinocchio doll. He was my favorite! He had a wooden head with a face painted in bright colors. He always looked happy, ready for adventures with me. His long lanky arms and legs attached to his body, all stuffed with cotton made him so easy to carry, to throw up and catch and to hug. He would flop down beside me for a nap anytime!

About eleven AM, long before Mama was ready to stop for lunch, I got hungry. "Mama, I'm hungry. When are we going to eat?"

"Not for a little while, you go on up to the house and get a banana. That will tide you over until I finish here."

I did as she said. On my way back as I was going up the ramp to the wharf over the rocks, the loose board moved. I lost my footing and fell down on the rocks screaming as I looked at the blood spurting out of my "skunned" knee. I remember wearing red shorts that day. Mama quickly put down the paint brush and ran to me.

"Well now, what happened here?" She saw the loose board, made from a barrel stave, separated from the others. "Come on, baby," she said as she gathered me up in her arms and carried me to the house. She fixed me up with her favorite remedy, mercurochrome. This interruption did not prevent her from finishing the task she had set for herself of painting the black part of the buoys. Finally she looked at me and said, "Now it's time for lunch. Bring Pinocchio and come along. We both need a break."

Daddy cleaned and dried the fish that he caught on the wharf. I loved to be around when he was doing that. Most of the time I played barefoot. The boned fillets looked so clean as he lined them up to dry. There were plenty of fishbones lying around. One day while he was working, I stepped on a bone. Not wanting to disturb him, I bit my lip and tried to pull it out myself. It hurt so bad that I finally screamed "Ouch!" Mama heard and came to me. She had me sit down right there. She leaned over and pressed with her left thumb right next to the bone that had gone up through the middle of my foot. With her right hand she took hold of the bone and pulled it out. So quick! No pain! I was astounded! "Mama, that didn't even hurt!" She said, "Let's go get some mercurochrome on that." She was my super mom. She could do anything!

During those years when I was six and seven, lobstermen used quart ginger ale bottles as "toggles" or floats for the traps with the wooden trap buoys. I used to play with the extra bottles they had saved. It was fun to crawl down over the rocky bank to the lobster pound to fill my bottles with water. Then I had plenty for doing my dishes and bathing my dolls. One day on my way back up to my playhouse with a wet full bottle in my hands I slipped. As I fell the bottle broke and cut my hand close to my wrist. Blood flew all over! I scrambled back up and ran to the house shouting, "Mama, Mama! I'm bleeding!"

She carefully took my hand and held it up in the air to get the bleeding to stop. She washed it good and this time used hydrogen peroxide to "get rid of all those germs!"

"Now hold still while I haul this together," she said as she tightly pulled and then taped the cut shut.

Mama didn't believe in stitches or running to doctors, then or now.

A real potential for danger in Mama's mind was bumblebees. She was scared to death of them. One day we were headed to school in our 40's blue Kaiser. I had the window down. As we were passing Slate Island, a big bumblebee flew in.

Mama screamed, "Get him out!" At the same time she jumped out while the car was running! Of course we stayed in the car! She ran alongside and said breathlessly, " I can't get back in until you get him out!" As she was running she reached in and got the car out of gear. She kept shouting, "Roll those windows down! Get that bee out!"

We finally did. She got in and drove on. We were a little bit late that day.

Johnny and I had a favorite game we played with bumblebees. They were easy to catch on fireweed blossoms. Using little peanut butter or marshmallow crème jars we caught several. When we thought we had enough, we dumped them into a gallon jar with water in it. We shook them around to get them all wet and then took them out to a ledge rock to set them free. It was fun to watch them get dry and fly away. One time

I sat on a bee to prove it wouldn't sting me. I was wrong.

Mama worked right along with Daddy on so many hard projects. Our one lane road was such an effort to maintain. Every year they bought some gravel to put in the worst places. Before putting in the gravel we would get mired down in honey holes. Johnny and I would jump out and get rocks or logs to fill up those holes. When they had a chance to get gravel from the pit across from the cemetery, Mama would pick us up from school in our second hand dump truck. Johnny was so excited about riding in it!

One time as she was getting ready to dump some on the bad spots, the tailgate wouldn't open. The cab, with Mama, Johnny and me in it went right up in the air!

Johnny yelled, "We're goin' up! We're goin' up!"

Daddy was there with the bulldozer ready to spread. He put the blade under the tailgate. Down we went.

Mama said, "Well, sir, now that was a ride, wasn't it?"

Daddy came to her window and said, "Are you all right, Marion? A few pieces of gravel wedged in the groove back there caused the problem. You go on. I'll be home for dinner as soon as I have this load spread. Johnny, do you want to stay with me?"

"Oh, yes, Daddy. Joan can go home with Mama."

Another job that Mama helped Daddy with was loading the lobsters into the truck. It wasn't too hard but always a bit dangerous because it was so slippery under foot. Unhooking the crate once, she lost her balance and flipped right out of the back of the truck. The hook caught into her heavy turtleneck and let her dangle!

"Elmer, get me down!" Mama yelled.

"It's OK, Marion, I'll have you off there in a minute. "Off" meant letting her down slowly into the water.

When she came out she was looking for her glasses which were still on her head.

To lighten the situation Daddy said, "Remember the time I lost mine leaning over the side of the boat? The next spring that big lobster came wearing them up to the head of the pound!"

It's a wonder that neither Johnny nor I got cut when we were playing "factory" using empty sardine cans. Daddy used to get his lobster bait at the Underwood Sardine Factory in Jonesport. Sometimes empty cans would accidentally be mixed in with the bait. Daddy saved them for us to use at our "packing plant." Johnny and I pretended we were selling cans of "specialties" we had packed ourselves. After gathering "winkles" for several days we dug out the meat and stuffed it, raw, into the tiny cans. We also picked the puffballs or little bladders off the rockweed that washed up. They were easy to press into the cans. The prettiest of all our "products" were the orange/red berries of the witchwood trees. Of course they were not ready until fall so our "factory" had a long season. Those tiny berries were so attractive in double layers in our bait cans. We were some proud of our products! We were even ready with our dried sand dollars to make change for our imaginary customers. What a line of them we had, waiting for cans of treasures from Black Duck Cove.

CHAPTER 3

Black Duck Cove was such an ideal place for us to live. It had everything: camping areas for people (from other states), very little traffic, the fascinating shoreline awash with tidal deposits and some pools big enough to play in safely. There was a forested area across the road. The Nature Conservancy owned the larger part of the Island. As children we never really wanted for anything; it was all right there!

The people who came for summer vacation enriched our lives. One family, the Baileys, came from New Jersey and usually stayed two weeks. Their red haired, freckle-faced daughter Junie was one year older than I so we played together every day. One of our favorite activities was to go out to the grassy knoll on the point. Cranberries, grass and bushes covered the area down to a sandy beach. When the tide was coming in and there was a little chop we would stand on the rocks and jump back as the tide surged. Of course as the rocks got wet, they also got slippery.

When we were playing out there one Sunday afternoon, Junie jumped back and yelled, "Watch out!" As I looked at her, I missed my own footing. I sat right down in the water! My red shorts and sneakers were soaked!

"Junie, what am I going to do? You know Mama doesn't want us out here anyway. She says it's too dangerous."

"Good thing they were all visiting when we left. They didn't even notice us."

"But what am I going to do? I'll really be in trouble if Mama sees these wet clothes!"

Junie calmly stated, "I'll go back to your house and get you some dry clothes and shoes. I'll sneak in so nobody will see me. Then you can change and go home dry as if this had never happened."

"But what will I do with these wet clothes?" I wailed.

"We'll just find a sunny stump in the woods where we can leave them to dry. Then tomorrow we'll come and get them," she declared as she headed back towards the house.

We followed her plan. It was lucky for me I had so many pairs of red shorts and another pair of shoes. Nobody paid any attention to us as we casually began playing around in the yard. The next day we retrieved the clothes which had dried, brought them home and put them in the clothes hamper unseen by Mama. She never knew! I got away with it!

The following Sunday afternoon Junie and I, carefree and bold, her pigtails bouncing, skipped back out to the forbidden knoll. We could not get enough of trying to beat the tide as it tried to make us lose our footing.

"Watch me!" I shouted to Junie as I was balancing on one foot. Just as fast as I said those words, I slipped and went all the way into the water, completely under, long hair and all!

As I came up shaking like a wet puppy, I exclaimed, "What ever am I going to do? It's Sunday and just a few hours before evening services."

Junie, my clever, older friend did not have a solution this time. "You'll just have to go home to get your hair washed to get all the salt and sand out of it. Maybe it will dry in time."

We plodded back home with no spring in our steps. I dreaded showing myself to Mama. I had disobeyed by going there and then by playing our "beat the tide" game on the slippery rocks on a Sunday afternoon! As we reached the door we could hear the voices of our happy parents chatting inside. My heart thumped so loudly I thought they would hear it before they saw me.

Mama jumped up when she saw her little girl looking like a drowned rat on the doorstep. "What have you done? No matter. You do not have to tell me. I can see that you have disobeyed.

You went out on the grassy knoll and you played on the rocks. You know you should not have done that. We do not have time to get your hair clean and dry before services. You are going to have to stay home tonight. You will not be going with us to church this evening, young lady."

She added to that punishment by telling me, "The next time Junie comes over you may not play outside."

Unfortunately, we had a forbidden place to play in the house too. Our attic did not have a floor, only beams sixteen inches apart with insulation on the sheet rock in between. Mama had boards across some of the beams where she stored her quilting materials. We knew how dangerous it was out there because one time Mama was reaching for a stack of quilt blocks, lost her balance and one leg went right down through the living room ceiling.

On Tuesday morning when Junie arrived (she had decided not to put in an appearance on Monday), Mama invited her in as if nothing had happened two days earlier.

"Hi, Junie!" I yelled from my playroom upstairs. "C'mon up!"

"Hi, Joanie, do you want to go outside?" Junie prompted, completely ignorant of my imposed punishment.

"Let's stay in today" I said, ashamed to tell her I had no choice when she was there.

"Well, what are we going to do? What are you doing?" she asked as she peered around the fully furnished playroom.

"Where does that door go?" she asked as she began walking toward it.

"That's our attic and we are not supposed to play in there. It is dangerous because there is no floor."

As I was finishing my sentence she put her hand on the knob and opened the door. The darkness of the attic was pierced by a shaft of light from the window at the opposite end.

"Ooh! This is spooky. Let's go in there. I want to see what's in there."

"No. We can't We could fall right down through the ceiling," I warned.

Junie looked at me as if I were two years old and countered, "We won't fall. We know how to be careful." With that she stepped out onto the beam where Mama's materials were and then began trying to walk the beams to the end of the attic. She missed. She fell completely through the ceiling into my father's easy chair in the living room.

Mama had gone out to the garden so didn't realize what had happened. Junie was not hurt but looked scared as she sprawled in the chair. I yelled, "I'm going to get the broom! Maybe we can get those tiles back up." Of course we couldn't. Junie had quickly left by the front door before Mama came in. When she did, I tearfully showed her what had happened. She said, "Thank the good Lord, Junie didn't get hurt. Your Daddy will have to fix that when he comes home."

I went back upstairs, closed the attic door and sat down in my playroom hoping that tomorrow Junie would want to play dolls.

CHAPTER 4

My playroom was great for rainy days in the spring or snowbound days in the winter. Since I loved to be outside, however, I had playhouses in all my favorite locations. The best thing about having playhouses at the homes of older relatives was that they gave me cast offs from their kitchens, like a dented bowl I could use as a dishpan or a nearly threadbare dish wipe that would dry quickly after use in my little kitchen. They saved little food boxes and cans for me to use too such as cocoa and baking powder cans, the boxes that kitchen matches came in and the occasional deviled ham can. I had so much fun arranging the items in or on empty shoe boxes and wooden cheese boxes that served as shelves and cupboards.

Della and Richard had a little cabin across the cove. On a lovely summer morning I would go into the kitchen where Mama was always busy at the stove.

"Mama, I want to go over to Della's today."

"That's fine. Be a good girl," she always said.

Johnny would go with me because he liked to play with his little boats in front of their camp at the head of the cove. We always carried a bell with us so Mama could hear us as we walked all the way around to Della's and Della would listen for our arrival.

"Well, children, come right in here and have a cookie and tea after that long walk," Della always said with a warm smile.

After a rest and a visit, we were ready to play outside all day. That would give Mama the whole day to help Daddy when she was done at the house.

One day the sissy boy who was staying next door to Della and Richard's cabin came running by my playhouse and grabbed my "new" dish wipe where it was drying on a bush. He just ran right off with it, round and round, up to the road and back down to the shore.

I was angry! He had teased me the whole time his family was there anyway. This time I followed him out to the road, grabbed a fist-sized rock and heaved it at him. Wow! It hit him dead center on the back of his head; he had to have lots of stitches. I could have killed the poor boy! I'm sure I did not realize the gravity of the situation at the time. I was just a little girl.

My punishment for that act was a strapping and no trips over to Della's for three weeks!

Those three weeks were not completely unhappy for me, however, because then I got to go to Aunt Myrtle's or Grammi Smith's on Beals. Actually my playhouse at Aunt Myrtle's really belonged to her daughter, Carolyn. Older than I, she had a lot of friends who invited her to their houses, so she didn't use her playhouse much anyway. It was filled with nice things that Carolyn had enjoyed alone or with me sometimes.

During my absence from Della when I was at Aunt Myrtle's my inner, hidden discontent must have spurred me to do a really awful thing! The one object I loved so in Carolyn's playhouse was her little flour sifter. When Mama came to pick me up one afternoon after grocery shopping, I decided to take the sifter home without a word to anybody. I knew it was wrong to take something that didn't belong to me, but I did it anyway. While Mama was still talking with Aunt Myrtle I went and hid it in the car. Then I just went back to play on the lawn.

"Come on, Joanie, it's time to go," Mama finally yelled from Aunt Myrtle's porch.

With my nicest manners I ran up to Aunt Myrtle, gave her a hug and said, "Thank you, Auntie, I had a wonderful time today."

"Bye Bye, honey. You can come back anytime. I am so glad you are enjoying Carolyn's playhouse."

We backed out of the driveway and headed home. As we drove across the new bridge I devised a plan to keep the flour sifter hidden from Mama: as soon as we got home, I would jump out and push it as far under the car as I could reach!

As Mama came back out from carrying in her first big bag of groceries, she said, "What is that under the car?"

I had not gotten it far enough under!

"Now where did you get that? Who gave it to you?" Mama questioned.

"I got it in Carolyn's playhouse," I sheepishly answered. Guilt must have been all over my face.

"Did she give it to you?" she demanded.

"Well, no, she wasn't there." Oh, how did I ever get myself into such a sorry situation?

Mama, probably wanting to grasp me firmly by my skinny little shoulders, said, "You'll take it right back and tell them you have stolen it out of the playhouse."

The very next morning, interrupting her work at home, Mama drove me over to Aunt Myrtle's. I could hardly keep from crying when Mama marched me right into that welcoming kitchen. Aunt Myrtle's smile slowly faded when she saw that the occasion was serious.

"Aunt Myrtle," I said as I held the little sifter up to her, "Yesterday I stole this out of Carolyn's playhouse. I'm sorry. I want to put it back."

Aunt Myrtle, my very favorite aunt in the whole world, chuckled softly before she said, "Well, dear, that's all right. You can have it because Carolyn doesn't play with it anymore. But your mother was right; you shouldn't take what doesn't belong to you."

Oh, what an experience! That confession was the hardest thing I ever had to do! I really loved Aunt Myrtle and my cousin Carolyn so much I never, ever, stole another thing!

I can't say the same for Johnny. One time we went to Bangor with Mama and Daddy. They had some shopping to do at a dry goods store, like a five and ten cent store. It was filled with delights for children: I got stuck on a monkey. It was as big as I was, big and brown! So realistic! It cost fourteen ninety-five.

"Look Mama! Look at that monkey! Can you get it for me?" I asked hopefully.

"No, dear, you can't have that. It costs too much," Mama stated softly as she guided me away.

Johnny, meanwhile, was wandering around in the stationary department looking at pens and tablets. He put a pen in his pocket unnoticed by anyone.

After we got home, Mama spied it. "Now where did you get this?"

Johnny replied, " In the store in Bangor."

Mama said "When we go to Bangor next time, you'll take it back."

Well, the next time they went to Bangor, we didn't get to go. Della and Richard went. Mama took the pen back to the dry goods store and came home with the monkey for me. I could not believe it! I was overjoyed! I named him Bobby Brinkley and kept him on my bed for years.

We didn't get a lot of lectures about right or wrong. We always went to Sunday School and church. Our most important lessons, however, we learned by being the children of parents with all the right values. Daddy was so honest in his work; Mama was always supportive of him and his work. They taught us by example that hard work and honesty brought their own rewards. Did they get the monkey for me because I did not steal anything from that store? Was it a way to teach Johnny a lesson? All I know is I'm glad I confessed to Aunt Myrtle about my theft of the flour sifter. And I was some happy with Bobby Brinkley.

Johnny and I had so much fun with fewer possessions than most kids had. In our playroom we amused ourselves for hours playing restaurant or school or church. Johnny was always the preacher and I was always the choir. One Christmas Daddy made us little desks and chairs so we could draw and color in the books that relatives gave us. Probably Johnny designed tree houses during one of those sessions.

CHAPTER 5

As children, Johnny and I were not intentionally mischievous, just adventurous. We really did not want to cause problems for our parents or depart from the values they were instilling in us. We just wanted to have fun. We were so isolated, especially before the bridge from Beals to Jonesport was built when I was eight years old in 1958. Until then M.I.Beal had a car ferry. He used a lobster boat attached to the ferry to push it across the Moosabec Reach to Jonesport. He and his son also used a lobster boat to carry foot passengers over. If we arrived at the wharf at low tide we had to climb up a ladder. I remember doing that but wonder how Mama did it with two little children in tow. Trips to the mainland were infrequent, often on an emergency basis.

Because we had only each other as playmates, Johnny and I were quite a team in imaginative play. We never considered the consequences when we jumped into a new adventure. We loved playing in the woods. Johnny felt so big cutting down small trees with a buck saw and a hand saw. Sometimes I used the buck saw when we were limbing them out. We worked and worked because Johnny the architect had planned a five story town house! In the woods!

One morning he started the day by coming to where I was burying a dead bird in my pet cemetery and said, "Let's build a tree house. We can get Daddy's saw, some nails and rope down at the wharf. He has plenty. Let's go."

One year and nine months older than I, Johnny had the ideas and I was always ready to go along with his schemes. "OK. I can carry the hammer and nails. I know where there is a coffee can we can carry them in."

"C'mon, then. Do you think there are some pieces of rope Daddy doesn't need?"

I thought a minute and then remembered seeing a pile of tangled pieces in the corner of the wharf shed. "Yes, I saw some down there just yesterday. A town house! Five stories! Can we do that?"

"Sure we can. First we will decide where to build it. We need a clearing where we can maybe use trees for cornerposts. We'll see."

Loaded down with all of our supplies we tramped from the wharf along the road skirting the Cove until we came to the path through bushy alders that we had made on numerous trips that spring and summer. In early June when the sun could still filter down through freshly leafed trees we made hammocks "to take sun baths" in.

Finally, Johnny exclaimed, "This is it! This is where we'll build our town house." It seemed he could always see the finished product his mind had created. I couldn't, but I trusted his leadership. He was my big brother.

"What should we do first?" I asked as we both dropped our loads at the base of a towering spruce.

"Well, Sister, I think I see just the spot for our house. Let's lay rope around the outside edge of where it will be. We'll use these trees for corners."

When we had laid out a rectangle that we could both fit in, Johnny said, "OK, now lets work on the other posts."

We set out to look for trees with two or three inch diameters, saplings. He used the hand saw and I used the buck saw. It didn't take us very long to get them down, limb them out and drag them back to our "foundation." Johnny used the hammer and then a sharp rock to dig the holes to stand the poles in. When he stood a pole down in a hole and held it straight, I filled in the hole with small rocks and dirt.

When the four corner posts were standing straight and tall, we got eight more skinny trees to use as cross members to hold the corners strong and steady. Johnny was good at nailing them together as I held above or below. Then we got more wood to use for the floor. When it was finished we walked around and around, back and forth, so pleased with our efforts.

Just as we heard Daddy's boat coming in to moor, Johnny said, "That's about it for today. Let's put all of our materials under this big tree, close to the trunk, so they will stay dry if it rains. Tomorrow we'll put up the walls for the first floor and then we'll just move on up."

"Johnny, how are we going to get the poles up so high?"

"Well, Sister, don't you worry about that; I'm making a winch to help us. You'll see."

We chatted excitedly all the way home. Our joy must have shown all over our faces because Daddy said when we sat down to supper, "Well, you two have certainly had a good day. What did you do?"

Johnny proudly replied, "We're building a tree house." That was all Johnny said and Daddy didn't pursue the subject. Somehow I knew Johnny didn't want me to blurt out all of his plans.

The next morning we could hardly wait to get back to the work. The first thing we did was gather brush to make the "walls." Then we gathered the rest of our materials and laid them out in rows by size. We both were pretty strong from carrying logs and from using ropes in other ways. We just kept on going up with the same idea that Johnny had for the first floor. One time I fell off the second floor but didn't get hurt at all. The forest floor was pretty soft there. Our ceilings were just a little higher than Johnny,so our five stories were completed before we knew it.

It was so much fun to be up on top, like in an eagle's nest on the mast of a schooner surveying our surroundings. We could see over our house to the flat rocks by the duck pond along the road about one half mile away. We could see the few cars coming and going along the road. On the Sunday afternoon following completion of our house, we were up there and saw George, a friend from church coming for a visit. The folks told him we were out in the woods in our tree house and how to get to it. He came and stood in awe looking up at us.

"Why, what have you two built here? I've never seen such a tree house!" George exclaimed.

Johnny was so proud and thrilled with the impact it had. He said, "We built ourselves the best tree house ever. It's our town house."

George said, "Has your Daddy seen it?"

I said, "No, he hasn't been out here yet."

George commented on the good job we had done, turned on his heel and very quickly left the scene.

He must have gone right back to the house and told Mama and Daddy about our spectacular tree house. In just a few minutes Daddy came through the woods with his saw. We watched him approach ready for compliments about our impressive architectural feat. Instead, he looked up at us and said, "You two have made something very dangerous. If you're not careful, you could fall right off, or the whole affair could tumble down. No sir, you can't be playing in such a dangerous place. Come on down."

We had no idea that he was going to remove the danger from us. He just sawed through all of our posts and down it came! Oh, how sorry we were! We had worked hard on it and had been careful as we played on it. But you know, our daddy never lectured us on using his materials and tools. He just wanted us to be safe. We understood that, but we were so sorry to lose our beautiful, unique five story tree house.

The very next day Johnny said, "While we still have the winch out there, let's make a cable car." We had seen ski lifts on T V. He chose two trees about fifty feet apart. We used one of the wooden lobster crates as a bucket. Johnny got it suspended about thirty feet high between the two trees. He was the operator; I was the passenger. He held the side of the crate steady while I got in.

Whee! I could just see myself flying through the air to the other tree. But no! Because the rope stretched with my weight, when Johnny pushed me off I made a vertical descent, straight to the ground. Nobody knew about this experiment but us.

When we were old enough Daddy built us each our own little skiff to use as lobster boats in our pound when it was empty in early summer. No project was too daunting for my brother's enthusiastic imagination or my willingness to be out on the water imitating my daddy. We used pick poles to push ourselves around the pound from trap to "trap," actually good sized rocks tied with a rope that we attached to a lath as a trap float. Our lobsters were wrinkles which would cling to the rocks; we had to haul them up easy so they wouldn't slide off. We also used green crabs as lobsters. Johnny built a pound for us with laths Daddy had taken off our old traps; it was about three by six feet around with the laths tightly placed side by side. We would go out and gather the green crabs and bring them back to our little pound. But when the tide came in, they would swim right out over the top. They were going for the lobster bait, so Daddy had to get rid of them. He made a grinder to grind them up; then we used rock shrimp. We were some tired at the end of a long summer day "hauling our traps." I never knew that one day Daddy would count on me, as Johnny had, to be his helper on the real lobster boat.

CHAPTER 6

Sometimes we used Daddy's boat for a very special experience on Black Duck Cove. When our good friends from New Jersey were there in the summer, we always planned a picnic out to Inner Ram Island. The party was composed of our friends with their two children, Della and Richard, our family and our two dogs, Blackie and Ripper.

As soon as we knew that our friends had arrived, I would watch for Daddy's return from hauling, "Daddy, Daddy, the Baileys are here! When can we go on a picnic?"

"Well, now, let me get out of these fishin' clothes and have some supper. Then I can think about your question." Daddy's reply was serious, but a smile played around his mouth and a twinkle shone in his eyes. It was almost as if he had seen their car while mooring and thought about our annual picnic with them too!

After supper Mama said, "Elmer, tomorrow looks like it will be pretty. What do you think about a picnic with the Baileys?"

Daddy replied in his steady voice, "Marion, I think a picnic tomorrow is a good idea."

Johnny and I were helping clear the dishes from the table when we heard that statement. We both put down what we were holding and ran to Daddy. "Really?" We both shouted at once. A picnic not only provided us with all the expected joys, but it gave us a chance to go out on Daddy's boat having fun with him and Mama.

We began preparing right after we finished the dishes. Mama baked a blueberry molasses cake, everyone's favorite. I counted out forks for the ten people and made sure that the picnic basket had plates, napkins and cups for all. I stood the two big thermoses by the stove; in the morning Mama would fill them with hot tea. We chose soda from the cartons in the cellar: strawberry, orange, grape, ginger ale and my favorite, Bubble Up. We would make a rock enclosure for them at the shore as soon as we arrived so they would be really cold at lunch time.

Sleep did not come quickly; it seemed like dawn would never come. Before daylight, the bellowing foghorn woke me up. My heart sank! I was some upset to think we might have to stay home!

I jumped out of bed, put on my bathing suit under my clothes and then ran downstairs to see if preparations were still being made, or had Mama and Daddy decided that the heavy fog would prevent safe passage out to the island? Daddy who surely knew Maine coastal fog assured me, "Don't worry darlin', this fog will be burned off by mid-morning."

While I helped Mama make the crabmeat sandwiches on homemade yeast bread, Daddy went out to get the boat and bring it in to the wharf. Johnny and I carried almost everything down to the wharf. At about ten AM Della and Richard saw us and joined us as did Junie and her family. After Johnny rounded up Blackie and Ripper, we all boarded the <u>Marion P.</u> Daddy attached the dinghy and we set out as the sun was breaking through for our wonderful day of picnicking on Inner Ram Island. Considering the tide, Daddy moored as close as he could.

"Yea! We're here!"

"We're here!"

"We're here!" All of us shouted at once. Blackie and Ripper added their barks of joy bringing smiles to everyone's faces.

Daddy said, "Well, come on you four and bring those dogs with you. You're my first passengers to shore."

The sun was shining now in bright blue, cloudless sky. Before Daddy had a chance to beach the dinghy, Blackie and Ripper jumped out and swam to shore. They were doing crazy runs, noses down for sea objects washed ashore and tails wagging as we ran to join them. Daddy yelled as he pulled away, "Now you're not going in swimming until I bring your Mamas in."

"OK, Daddy, we won't," Johnny yelled in his strongest voice.

It seemed like forever until they arrived, all laden with the picnic provisions. Richard and Mr. Bailey secured the sodas in the little coastal rock enclosure to get them good and cold. The women put everything down and then Mama yelled out, "Swim time!"

We threw off our clothes and ran out on the sandy beach into the sun warmed ocean. Oh the fun we had jumping and running, swimming and splashing! We had races and throwing the stick contests for the dogs to retrieve. We would have stayed until dusk doing all that, but sooner than we wanted Mama motioned for us to come to lunch. Blackie and Ripper had to be stopped before they neared the refreshments to shake the water off their coats. Johnny and I gave them their "picnic biscuits" and then we all settled for the tasty food Mama and I had prepared the night before. I guess there is nothing more delicious than crabmeat sandwiches washed down with soda and blueberry molasses cake followed by hot tea.

After lunch we decided to build a huge sand castle. Johnny loved planning the whole project. I loved going down to the water to bring back pails of wet sand to use for "cement." Finally at three PM Daddy yelled, "Time to gather up. We need to start for home now."

When we got back to our wharf, Mama had us take off our shoes to dump out the sand. She brushed the rest off as best she could. We left the sand there but carried the memories of that beautiful summer picnic in our hearts and minds like treasures from the sea.

"Uuoo, uuoo, uuoo," The sound of the foghorn pulled me out of my reveries. I looked at my watch and asked Daddy, "Is that our lunch signal?"

Daddy had just pulled away from the last trap in the string which had yielded two keeper lobsters, one crab, and a lovely little flatfish. I had no idea that the morning had passed while I had been in my playhouses, building the tree house with Johnny and on our picnic. Remembering the delicious lunch we had that day really worked up my appetite.

"I'd say so," Daddy replied.

We both went back to the stern and settled down on the empty crates with blankets on them that we used for seats. Oh, it felt so good to take the weight off our feet, to flex our knees and to look around to loosen our neck muscles. Lobstering is very strenuous work, but it is what we know and love. Daddy's skill with my help makes a good living for us, but oh, how tired we get!

"Here's your sandwiches, Daddy. I was just remembering that beautiful picnic we had with Della and Richard, the Baileys, Blackie and Ripper. Just think, they are all gone, but the memories of all we did that day including the lunch are still with me. Do you recall what else we had for lunch that day, Daddy?"

"I sure do: sandwiches just like these on your Mama's homemade bread and her wonderful blueberry molasses cake for dessert. Where's our dessert today?" He smiled knowing that she or I would have tucked in something sweet.

"How about that bread she used to bake, the length of a cookie sheet? It was over an inch thick. She used to cut slabs of it to toast for our breakfast. Johnny and I would fill up on that every morning, spreading it thickly with homemade jelly. Johnny's favorite was apple; mine was grape. What was yours, Daddy?"

"Now you don't ever have to ask me that. Her strawberry jam was and still is my favorite. You and I used to pick strawberries at that farm near church camp in New Brunswick. When we went to pay for our harvest we always told the lady we had probably eaten a box between us as we picked."

"Oh, yes. She always told us we didn't have to pay for the ones already in our stomachs. They were so sweet and juicy, perfect for jam. Mama used to carry along to camp all her jelly making equipment so she could make preserve that summer for us to enjoy all winter. It was some tasty!"

Daddy rejoined, "And remember the Bake-Apples (Cloudberrys) we would pick, up on the heath? Oh, how she worked jarring those to have for pies in the winter."

"Yes," I said, "But we also had crab apples that we picked from the old deserted orchard down at the sand cove. Of course we dried some and stored plenty to eat raw in the winter too. They never had quite the flavor that they had in autumn. But oh, those pies!"

"Now my favorite pie was your Mama's mincemeat. You know Marion and I loved to go birdin' but we also went out for deer. Usually we each got one. She used venison in her mincemeat. She really knew how to grind up that deer meat along with dried apples and raisins, brown sugar and that dried orange peel. The spices she mixed in as she was preparing to jar it made the whole house smell good! There was nothing better than a piece of her pie with homemade ice cream on it."

"Your homemade ice cream was the best. I knew what my part was in that project! Johnny and I chipped up ice outside while Mama was cooking that creamy custard on the stove. When it was cooked and cooled a bit, you would pour it into the freezer canister and put the chopped ice all around it. Then you took it down cellar to turn that handle."

" I also remember how many times you would holler down the stairs, 'Is it froze yet?' When I couldn't turn the handle any more, I would lift the canister out and come up to the kitchen. Your mama would pull out the dasher and lay it on a platter. She cleaned it off with a spoon."

"Yes, and then Johnny and I used spoons to quickly clean off the platter before melting occurred. We got the first taste. It was some good!"

" When you were about eleven years old, your Mama taught you how to cook and bake. You became quite a pie and cake baker."

I was so pleased that he enjoyed some of my kitchen triumphs. I learned how to make lemon meringue, lemon sponge and walnut pies. She taught me how to bake molasses and sugar cakes and homemade yeast bread. On Saturdays when Mama was down at our pound buying lobsters from other fishermen for our pound, I had to do all of my chores as well as the baking. It was a chore back then. I made four loaves of bread at a time. It had to rise twice and then be rolled out and put in loaf pans where it had to rise again before being put in the oven. The whole project took six to seven hours.

"Well, Daddy, I'm glad Mama taught me how to be a success in the kitchen. And I'm really glad you taught me how to help you and do most everything on the boat."

"You're the best sternman I could ever have. Now let's get back to work."

As we took our positions, Daddy pulled on to the next trap buoy but my mind captured one more fond memory, popcorn.

We enjoyed popcorn on long winter evenings also. Mama had a high sided hot dog steamer that she would put the oil and kernels in. We took turns shaking the pan back and forth over the burner listening for it to pop and then to stop popping. We all had separate bowls that we would fill and take with us to our game or book or a puzzle. One evening when Richard and Della were staying with us, Richard took his bowl upstairs to enjoy while he was reading alone. Guest bedrooms were directly over part of the living room. Daddy decided to clean his gun while he was eating from his bowl. Of course he thought all the shells were out of it. He was sighting the gun while aiming it at Johnny's paper airplane hanging down by a thread in one corner of the living room. Having the sight just perfect, he pulled the trigger: "Boom!" The gun was not empty! The shot went right through the plane bringing it down and through the ceiling whizzing past Richard in his reading chair!

"What's happening down there?" Richard shouted.

We all went upstairs to be sure he was OK and Daddy found the shot hole in the wall. Since no one was hurt, we all laughed but Johnny nearly cried as he picked up the pieces of tissue and balsa wood from the shattered model plane on the floor.

That experience did not deter Richard from participating in our family life, especially in the winter. We loved having them with us, just as if our real grandparents lived with us.

Richard helped Daddy with a lot of the winter chores, as we all did. Daddy made many trips into the woods to haul wood to earn money. Money was tight in the winter so this was one way he earned some extra. He used to let me go with him. With his bulldozer he pulled a sled that held two cords. After he cut a tree and limbed it out, he let me carry the chunks I could lift over to the sled.

"Daddy, how about this one? Can I take it?" I would call time after time.

"That one looks about right. You take it right on over to that sled."

About noon on those days in the wintry woods we would hear the engine of our jeep approaching. "Here comes Mama! Look! Richard's in the back!"

Daddy shouted to me, "I see them. I'm some hungry. I hope she has enough for all of us!"

Mama turned the jeep around and then stopped. There was Richard sitting on the floor in the back holding a big pot of meat soup. I climbed into the back with him.

"That sure smells good, Marion!" Daddy exclaimed as he climbed in the front with Mama. She opened up her picnic basket and pulled out buttered biscuits, wrapped in towels to keep warm, a molasses cake and tea. Nothing ever tasted any better there in the woods in the winter!

CHAPTER 7

As Daddy and I went through the afternoon, hauling, emptying and resetting traps, my mind returned to memories made and now cherished. Remembering that incident of the popcorn brought back winters from my childhood. Evenings with popcorn and homemade ice cream always followed days of fun in the snow.

We usually got a lot of deep snow in those days. One winter we had eight foot deep drifts! Johnny loved to shovel snow and that winter he surely had a lot of chances to do it.

When we woke up, practically snowbound the morning after the big fall, Johnny exclaimed as he stared out the window, "Today I think we'll make a tunnel. We can go straight from the door, down across the yard to the road."

"How will we ever make a tunnel that long?" I asked, knowing well he would have a great answer for me . He always had an answer for my questions, whether I asked or not.

"I will start digging and we will put the snow in a crate on our sled. You can haul it out and dump it somewhere. That way it won't pile up inside, OK?"

He really didn't expect an answer from me; instead we just turned to the business of getting into our snow pants, jackets, caps and mittens. We brought up a box from the cellar to put on the sled. We were glad we had left it standing against the side of the house beside the door. The shovel was there too.

"Let's go," Johnny said as he threw the first shovel full of the snow into the box. It was fun to watch the tunnel develop and really hard to pull that loaded sled back out to the entrance. It took us two days to dig it from the house all the way down the hill and along the road.

When it was finished, Johnny said to Daddy at supper, "Can we spray water onto the floor of our tunnel to make it good for sliding?"

Daddy thought a while, probably weighing the possibilities for any danger at all if we did that. "I think that would work," he directed to Johnny, trying to give Mama a look of assurance at the same time. He knew Mama would worry about accidents since she had experienced so many with us.

Daddy himself brought the hose up from the cellar where it was kept in the winter. He attached it to the kitchen sink and then stepped out the door almost into the entrance of our wonderful tunnel. He pulled the hose behind him and went in the tunnel way down to the end to begin spraying on the snow floor. When he got back up to the entrance he said, "There now; you're going to have a good slide in the morning!"

"Thank you, Daddy!" Johnny and I both said. We knew it would take too long for the night to pass!

Sure enough, we flew through that tunnel over and over the next day and the next and the next. It was one of the best of our winter creations.

Later on when there was still a lot of snow, we built a horse. He was almost life sized with a thick, sturdy body and legs. We threw a blanket across his back so we could ride him in place!

We loved playing in the woods in the snow too. We took turns making tracks for the other to follow. Blackie and Ripper were so fast at following to the hidden destination that it really wasn't the game we had planned.

Blackie and Ripper also loved to ride on our sleds with us, especially Blackie. He just sat right up in the front as if he were the one choosing the way to go! He really loved our Bob-o-Link sled, as did we! It was a two seater and had a steering wheel. It had runners, like skis. Our road was so narrow and steep that we really went fast; we had no worry about cars in the winter! One day in the second year with the sled, rain came and made the road so rutty that it was very hard to steer. With Blackie in the front, Johnny steering and me in the rear, we started down the uneven surface still at a goodly speed. Finally, just as we came to the crossing we lost control. Blackie jumped off and we crashed; we stove it up beyond repair. It was good we still had our Western Flyers!

It was a good thing that the only traffic on our road in the winter was from our own jeep, truck, tractor or bulldozer. Daddy was the one who maintained the road in all seasons. In the winter even though he kept it plowed, we sometimes had to contend with ice.

One time when Mama and I were in the jeep carrying Daddy's lunch out to him, we had to drive over some ice. We broke right through and Mama had to winch us out. Another time Daddy was driving us to school. We hit a patch of ice and started to slide out of control. Johnny yelled, "Oh, here we go! Here we go! We're going down the bank." Sure enough we did but got stopped by a bushy bunch of alders. Daddy had to get out on the passenger side but then winched us out of the place where we had slid to a stop.

One icy Sunday morning it was very difficult to get up Deep Cove Road. Coming down the other side, a glare of ice all the way, our jeep began to really slide. Daddy let it go because he couldn't control it anyway. At the bottom we couldn't make the corner, so we drove right into the woods. Johnny was scared to death and so excited. "Watch out for the trees, Daddy!" he screamed.

All of a sudden we stopped. Daddy put the jeep into four wheel drive, backed up until he could turn around and then drove right out onto the road. We got to Sunday School on time!

We went through a lot of hardships to live out on Great Wass; however, Mama and Daddy loved it so much, that they would go through anything. Because we were the only family on the road, Daddy took complete care of the dirt roads which were so demanding: ice and snow in winter, mud in spring, and potholes at every season. Mama became an expert with the winch. Daddy had fun with the bulldozer too. He and Bud Moore, a man who worked for Daddy, would use it to get down to the cape shore to go birdin'. One winter they went right across the three heaths, got to the shore, shot the birds and then came really fast back across the heath. Daddy just opened her up! Bud was sitting on top holding the guns. They had tied the birds to the blade. What a sight they made racing into the yard at dusk.

Sometimes we had those birds for Christmas dinner, a few Mama didn't have to jar. In those years we didn't have a freezer so everything was either jarred or dried or eaten fresh. We always had something good to eat.

My memories of Christmas, however, do not center around food. They are of presents and Santa. When Aunt Eleanor and Uncle Franklin were with us one winter he dressed up as Santa for us. We had never seen a Santa before like children in the cities had. When he came in on Christmas Eve, Johnny immediately blurted out, "Where are your reindeer?"

He replied, "I left them up on the flat rocks with the sleigh."

"Well, I want to see them. I want to give them some carrots to eat," Johnny begged.

Mama quickly retorted, "No, those reindeer might bite you."

Daddy said, "And now, you children better go off to bed so Santa can fill your stockings."

"OK, Merry Christmas, Santa. See you next year!" I said as we climbed the stairs.

Then the year that I was seven at Christmas time and Johnny was almost nine, Mama told us about Santa. She told us that somebody long ago made up the idea of Santa. She wanted us to realize that the real reason for gifts and celebrations was because God gave the greatest gift of all, His Son, Jesus on Christmas Day. We grew up loving the true Christmas story and especially when the angel talked about the "Tidings of great joy." I thought that those were especially for us; we lived by the tides.

And so on Christmas Eve when we went up to bed, Mama and Daddy really got busy finishing up their plans for us. Sometimes there were rooms we were forbidden from entering for days before Christmas. The year that Johnny got the train he wanted Daddy to set it up on a table in the playroom. After we had "picked the tree" that Christmas Eve, Daddy said, "Let's go up to your playroom now." When he opened the door he said, "Johnny Beal, what have you got now?" Oh, Johnny was so happy. That was such a wonderful gift to him but for both of us to enjoy. We set it up so that the tracks went all the way from his bedroom into mine under our beds and back out. What fun we had! Our little freight train ran for hours with us loading and unloading important shipments, like the things we sold from our factory in the summer.

We really stayed busy in those days after Christmas with unique gifts Mama and Daddy chose for us. The relatives always gave us new materials for writing or art work: thick tablets with one hundred pages of fresh paper, coloring books, animals, trucks and boats to become our own creations. Fresh boxes of long crayons, pencils with good erasers and flat tins of paints with skinny brushes kept us developing our talents and skills year after year.

One Christmas Eve after we had "picked the tree," that is, removed and opened all the gifts that had been put under it, Daddy smiled so big. He could hardly wait for us to see what he had been working on for weeks in the cellar. When we thought he was down there building wooden traps, he was really constructing surprises for us.

He said, "You go up to your playroom." We did and saw nothing new. That's because when we went up, Daddy went down to bring our gifts up from the cellar to put in front of the tree.

"OK. Come on down!" Daddy announced.

We scrambled down and into the living room, trying not to fall over each other in our excitement. We were speechless when we saw what was shining so proudly there beneath the tree. There were two beautifully varnished little desks with four cubby holes, two drawers on one side and one across our knees all with silver knobs! One for each of us! We could hardly wait to arrange our new writing materials in them.

"Daddy, I just love it!" I said as I ran over to hug him.

Johnny said, "I'm going to keep my new crayons and pencils in the cubby holes, right here." He immediately stashed them away and then put his new color books and tablets in the drawers.

On Christmas Day Daddy carried them up to our playroom. They smelled so good and were so smooth to work on. We stayed there the whole day, except for eating dinner.

At another Christmas time, when I was seven years old, Mama and Daddy were going to Bangor to Christmas shop on Christmas Eve day. Because Johnny already had a little red wagon, I wanted one too all my own. It was all I wanted! We stayed home that day with Della and Richard. When they got home, Daddy came in alone and said, "Now don't watch us unload the car. You might see something you shouldn't."

Richard said, "OK, Elmer. Come on in, Joan; come in, Johnny. Let's go up to your playroom."

They hauled everything into their bedroom. When Mama and Della were getting supper and Richard and Daddy were visiting in the living room, I ran right into their bedroom. There was the big box with Radio Flyer on it. They had gotten it! Oh how I wanted to run to them screaming with joy, "You got it!" but I didn't let on. Ever.

They had us go upstairs again while they were putting gifts in front of the tree. Finally they called us down. There it was! Out of the box! Daddy had made a skiff for Johnny so he was just as thrilled. No, he couldn't have been. My joy made up for and hid my lack of surprise!

I put all of my gifts in the wagon and began going around and around in the house. I even put Blackie in it. He loved sharing my fun! I wore everybody out that Christmas until finally Daddy said, "Well, now it's time to let your new wagon rest. Tomorrow it is going to have to be ready to do some work helping me."

"OK, Daddy." I said. "Thank you for my wagon. I love it!"

I went up to bed and fell asleep imagining pulling it all around loaded with rope or tools to help Daddy. "What..." I wondered as my mind shut down, "Would a trap fit on it sideways?"

The years of the train and the wagon must have followed good seasons of fishing because we learned later that the train cost fifty dollars. The desks did not cost as much in money, just more in Daddy's labor. One Christmas was very lean, by contrast. With almost no money for gifts, Mama's ingenuity and effort really shone. She dug my discarded Pinocchio doll out of the toy box and said, "I'm going to put this little boy up in the attic; he's all worn out." I had put him aside when one arm lost its stuffing and his painted face had lost its happy expression. She actually took it to her room. Hidden from me, working at night, Mama recycled Pinocchio! She carefully made and painted a new cloth face, restuffed his arms and legs and made him a cute new little outfit. Johnny's favorite soft toy at that time had been a stuffed lion, the "lookingest thing you ever saw." It was all dilapidated and rather dirty. Mama got some new furry cloth and completely redid that lion, like sewing him up in a new snow suit! We were some proud of our old worn out toys made new.

Mama was so handy when it came to sewing. For me her best creations were her quilts. She saved all of our old clothes, ones that we couldn't wear anymore. In the winter she tore them apart and cut squares from the least worn parts of them. She sewed them together to make quilt tops. She used old sheet blankets for the filler and then new but cheap cotton cloth for the backs. She laid the three layers all out on the kitchen floor. Using a big darning needle and crochet thread she knotted them all together. It made me feel important to help her with the knotting. Together we made two or three every winter. How I loved to snuggle under Mama's homemade quilts – and I still do!

One winter Sunday night when we got home from church Mama had tucked me in early because I had a cold. I drifted off thinking about the movie we had seen at church about the Rapture. Suddenly noises outside and a very bright light shining in my eyes woke me up. "It's the Rapture!" I thought. I jumped out of bed and ran to Mama and Daddy's bedroom. Their bed was empty! They had already been taken! I ran to Johnny's; he was not there either! "They've all been taken and I've been left behind!" My eyes were filling with tears and my heart was pounding as I ran downstairs to the kitchen. When I looked out the window, there in the bright light of a full moon, Mama, Daddy, Johnny and two workers were putting out the ice down at the pound.

What a blessed relief it was to my frightened soul to see all of them working at one of the things Johnny and I loved most, putting out the ice. With no thought at all about my cold, I quickly got myself rigged up and out to help. Daddy had already done the cutting of the ice in the pound into ten to twelve foot wide strips, sometimes the length of the pound. He had strung rope from one end of the pound, by the gates, to the other end.

As I reached the end opposite the gates, Johnny yelled, "Come on, Sister! Jump on!" He was already holding onto the rope; I grabbed it as I jumped on. We were on our way riding the ice out to the other end where the workers were by the gates with pick poles to push the ice strips out into the cove. There had to be a high tide and easterly wind to float the ice out to sea.

That night when Johnny reached the gates he didn't jump back onto another float in time, so he went riding straight out into the cove! All the adults were so busy keeping their eyes on their own jobs that they did not notice him. All of a sudden he shouted hysterically, "Daddy, Daddy, I'm going out into the cove and I can't get back! The ice is breaking up under my feet!"

Daddy quickly ran precariously across the ice to the motorboat, jumped in and chased the ice Johnny was riding straight out to sea. "Here you go, Son; jump in here," Daddy said as he pulled alongside Johnny's raft.

"Thank you Daddy. I'm some glad to be in this boat! You saved my life!" Johnny exclaimed through chattering teeth. "I'm all done helping tonight."

"Well, Son, this is a dangerous business, but I know you are big enough to help. You just have to keep your mind on what you are doing."

Daddy brought him safely home. Mama said, "That's enough help from these children tonight. Joanie, you should not even be out here. Now you two go in, get warm and go to bed."

Crawling back under my quilt that night was a real comfort. Mama and Daddy and Johnny were still here. I was not left alone after all.

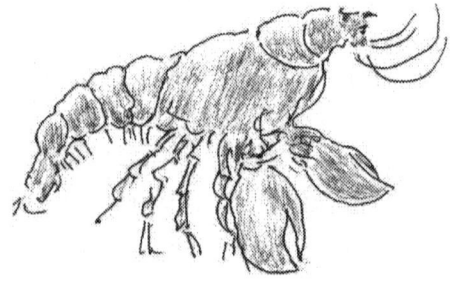

CHAPTER 8

The day passed as Daddy and I went from trap to trap, finally pulling up the last one. It looked like the barrels would yield about three hundred lobsters, a good haul for a fine summer day.

"Well, Daddy, what kind of a haul do you think we made today?" I shouted as I began to clean up the stern.

"Looks to me like nearly three hundred, a good day I'd say," Daddy replied as he turned towards Beals Island, where a longtime friend would buy his catch and fill up the gas tank. When the lobster was all taken care of, Daddy got four pails of bait to start with early the next morning.

As he pulled away headed for our mooring and the skiff, I thought aloud, "Why don't you and Mama join me for dinner tonight? I put a stew in the crock pot this morning before I left. Tell Mama to bring some bread."

"That sounds good to me," he said. He knew Mama would welcome the chance to eat at my table. Since Johnny had left for New York that morning it would just be the three of us. We ate a lot of fish, which we loved, but a savory beef stew always satisfied us. The meat, carrots, potatoes, onions and turnips seasoned with basil, parsley and thyme would surely be at their tasty best when we were ready to sit down.

He pulled into our mooring spot and we both got down into the skiff to go to the wharf. The gulls who had been cleaning up after us all day finally stopped circling and just landed on the shore rocks and on the wharf to check for washed up or dropped food there. What scavengers! But I loved them! They have always been a part of my life and I guess a symbol of Daddy's success at sea.

"See you soon," I said as I gave him a quick kiss good-bye.

"Give me an hour to clean up and we'll be there!" He smiled as he walked towards his truck.

I climbed up the path to my house enjoying my gardens, the birds feeding and the squirrels scampering off the deck as I let myself in. The whole house was filled with the scents of the stew. Leaving my fishing clothes by the washer, I went in to have a hot shower before putting on clean jeans and shirt for supper. I put on the kettle for tea, set the table and then went out on the deck to rest. They would be here in about thirty minutes.

It is so pleasant to sit outside as the day comes to an end. It had been a long and hard, but typical, day for Daddy and me on the <u>Marion P.</u> High summer is the best time for the richest harvests. Buyers are always pleased when Daddy comes in with a barrel or more of shedders. Shedders are lobsters that have molted their hard outer skins and are in the process of growing fresh, new shells. Of course there is always a high market for the hard shelled ones too, especially if they are fat two-pounders. Oceanside restaurants usually offer both types on the menus. At home we eat what's left, the firmer fleshed hard shelled or the shedders.

Besides the lobsters that Daddy and I have fished for together nearly forty years, we also bring home a lot of eel grass crabs and rock crabs. Mama's job is to steam them and then carefully pick out all of the sweet meat. She packs it tightly in one pound containers sometimes selling it to the summer cottage folk but daily making crabmeat sandwiches for all of us. There truly is nothing tastier than a heap of crabmeat on a slab of homemade buttered bread.

Oh, here they come now and I can see that Mama has a loaf of bread in foil.

"Hi Mama, Daddy. Come on in. Are you as hungry as I am?"

"You know your Daddy is," exclaimed Mama, " and I'm ready to eat too. Here's a loaf of bread to go with your stew. I just took it out of the oven."

I dished up the stew, we sat down and then we all bowed our heads.

Daddy intoned, "Lord, we are thankful for the good day you gave us and for this good food you provided for us. Thank you for the hands that prepared it and bless us as we eat it that we may grow stronger to serve you better. In Jesus' name, Amen."

After we had all eaten several helpings, I got up to pour the tea which had been steeping in my pretty old teapot from Grammi Smith. By now the sun was sinking lower in a cloudless sky filling my dining room with the orange afterglow of a beautiful day.

As we sipped our tea, I said, "Mama, I have had the most wonderful day remembering special times of my childhood. I remembered that time Daddy shot down Johnny's model plane and nearly scared Richard off his chair upstairs. Remember that?"

"Of course! How about that day at the end of winter when I was getting an early start on the spring cleaning? I had the pictures off the walls and the couch pulled out to the middle of the room. You thought that was fun because you were closer to watch the cartoons on TV."

Daddy said, "Oh, I remember what happened there! It was terrible."

"It was." I interrupted. "When we heard the thud of the door...!"

Our cellar door was a four by four trap door with a hook on top to attach to the wall to hold it up. It was huge, double thickness; Mama had a big job lifting it up and hooking it. That morning she just propped it, not hooking it. Our big Lab, Blackie, came running through and knocked the door down when she was on the steps!

"Oh, Mama, we heard the thud, we heard you stumbling and the empty bucket bouncing down the steps!"

"I was just outside bringing in a pail of lobster from the pound when I heard you scream, Joan." Daddy recalled. "I remember running as fast as I could to pull that door up and hook it before going down those steps to get you, Marion dear."

"Oh my how that hurt when it hit me on the top back of my head. I saw stars! Luckily I was just four steps from the bottom, not too far to fall." Mama sighed with a heavy breath almost as she had when she sat dazed on the cellar floor.

"You had a headache for days, but thank the good Lord, no permanent damage," Daddy rejoined. "And what a blessing it never fell on me when I used to go up and down putting wood in the furnace three times a day. Do you know how Uncle Franklin and I devised a way to get wood from the wharf to the house?"

"Yes," I said. "I always wanted to ride in that box that you put the wood in and pulled up to the house on a pulley."

"I know you did, Darlin', but that was a back breaker as it was," Daddy answered. "You were a big help, though, getting the boughs from the spruce trees and branching them out. Do you remember the steam box I attached to the furnace to steam those boughs and bend them for the rounded tops of our old wooden traps?"

"Yes, Daddy; the scent from that steam freshened the whole house."

"Well, Darlin', we had some hard times when you were a little girl, but we made it and now we can just remember," Daddy mused.

"Joan, how about way back when you were only three years old the day you were preparing a tea party with your little green plastic tea set?"

"Oh, yes, you had been getting ready to go to town. When you called me I put my little tea pot in the oven to keep it hot until we got home."

"Yes, and when we got home, what a smell greeted us as we opened the kitchen door!" Mama said.

"There was my little tea pot in a big green slab on the bottom of the oven! I was crying my teeth out when I saw that."

"I thought you had burned yourself," Mama replied.

"No, I was just so upset at losing one of my cherished toys. At the time I was not aware of the hard time you were going to have scraping that out."

"Actually, it took days. I couldn't use the oven in that old oil burning stove until the plastic was gone. What a mess that was!"

"Luckily you could still use the top burners. That was how you heated the water to do the laundry, wasn't it? First, you would pump the water up from the well into the holding tank, isn't that right?" I asked.

Daddy said, "I would try to get that done before heading out for the day."

"And you heated the water in a ten gallon oval copper tub on the two burners, didn't you?" I asked.

"Yes," said Mama. "We heated it and poured it into the wash tub on wooden chairs. Then we got the generator and could make electricity when needed. I got a wringer washer. Do you remember that, Joan?"

"Yes. When you put the clothes through the wringer they fell into the rinse tub. Then we put them back through to get the rinse water out. My job was to hand them to you."

Mama said, "And then you got to hand them to me right by the door where your Daddy had installed a pulley clothes line. You were a big help, dear."

Daddy said, "Life got so much better when we got that lighting plant, our generator. Oh, yes sir, that was one of the best purchases we ever made!"

"Yes, Elmer, and how about the day we almost burned it up?"

"Oh, yes. I remember! Richard and I were in the generator shed working on traps. It was very chilly that early spring day so we had a fire in the little wood stove."

We had hardly sat down for lunch up at the house when Richard said, "I smell smoke." We knew it wasn't from the meat soup and biscuits we were eating.

"I remember looking out and seeing the shed roof on fire," Daddy said.

"You ran out like a scared rabbit, Daddy! Johnny, Della, Mama and I followed, grabbing buckets along the way," I recalled.

"Elmer, you grabbed an ax, jumped up on that roof that was already on fire and began chopping out the burning cedar shingles. Richard handed up the buckets of water that the rest of us were filling and lugging up as fast as we could. Oh my goodness! Have we ever worked so fast? We knew we had to save our lighting plant!" Mama recalled with passion.

"Well, Daddy, you always were and still are great in an emergency!"

"Saving that generator with everyone's help probably made us appreciate it even more," Daddy said.

"So many things have changed in our lives and in this house. Remember how small it was at first? We just had the cellar and the two rooms downstairs and two bedrooms above. I don't know what made me think of this but I guess it was recalling our bedrooms upstairs. You had mine fixed up so cute, Mama. At school we were studying history of how the early statesmen used quill pens for signing their names to those important documents. I could hardly wait to get home that day to try it myself using a gull feather. I knew you had ink, Mama, so I sneaked out the little bottle from upstairs. When I was trying so hard to make it work, I accidentally knocked the bottle over. It went all over my pretty little rug. Did I say I was sorry, Mama?"

"Yes you did, and I told you never to touch the ink again."

We all laughed and then, relaxed and warmed from our evening of reminiscing, Daddy said, "We've certainly had our share of hard work and of joy together. I think I'd like to go home and go to bed now, a very happy man. Come on, Marion dear, tomorrow will be here before we know it."

I quickly washed the dishes and put them to drain before falling into bed myself. My quick prayer was, "Thank you, Lord, for the most wonderful mother and father a woman could have. Amen."

CHAPTER 9

Drifting off to sleep after spending the evening with Mama and Daddy caused me to wake up the next morning still thinking about friends and relatives. Of course my Grammi and Grampy Smith were my heroes. Grammi was a real nanny type. She always played with us down on the floor. She must have done that often because Mama was one of eight children raised in the two room house sleeping three to a bed. Oh how I loved that humble little cottage!

Grammi did not even have electricity until the sixties; she cooked on a big old-fashioned wood stove. Every time we went there after school on the bus she had a cookie jar filled with molasses and sugar cookies. If she didn't have cookies, she had a sugar cake with fancy swirled chocolate frosting. She always gave us a big hunk. It was some yummy! Sometimes she had a molasses cake or a blueberry molasses, the same recipe Mama uses today.

After we had had our treats, she would let me go out to gather eggs in the hen house. Her dog Timmy was the guard on duty out there.

One day as I went out with the little basket, Grammi said, "Be careful now. You know the rooster is cranky."

"I will," I said, feeling so important with my assignment. Well sir, that rooster jumped right on my back after I had picked three or four eggs out of the nest boxes on the floor. I hollered for dear life and ran right back outside

Grammi saw me coming, screaming with the empty egg basket jumping around in my hand. "What happened?"

"The rooster got me!" I cried.

"Where are your eggs, Darlin'?" she gently queried. She needed those eggs but never made me feel bad that I had dropped the basket and they had all rolled out and broken.

Timmy came running after me too as if to scold me for the whole episode. I decided right then that Timmy and the rooster would never see me trying to get eggs away from their hens again!

Grammi's yard was so beautiful with a large flower garden. It was a big square on the lower part of the yard enclosed in a white picket fence. She had dahlias, glads, marigolds and nasturtiums. She let me pick bouquets to take into the house. Her gardens surely awakened in me an early love for flowers At home I planted nasturtiums and glads. One time I had the base of an old stove, five feet square and one foot deep. I planted it full of orange and yellow nasturtiums. They were spectacular spilling over the sides. I always picked the seeds. I also had a little spot along the driveway with twenty-five to fifty glads and dahlias. I wanted our house to be as charming as Grammi's.

There was a lady, Mrs. Dory, who came around in the spring with little packets of vegetable and flower seeds. She was a tall stocky woman with a weathered complexion and red hair who always had a story to accompany her sales. I loved listening to her as I looked through the little packets.

Finally she would ask, "And what have you chosen today?"

One time I varied from the morning glories, zinnias, sunflowers and nasturtiums. I said, "I want radishes and beets."

After tending them carefully from planting to harvest, they both produced good crops. Mama cooked the greens and jarred the beets she pickled. I was proud of my choices that summer when I had just finished the fourth grade.

Now as I return home from a hard day of hauling or from a trip to Jonesport for groceries, I am thrilled to see my present day efforts enhancing my home with beauty. Sometimes during a really cold spring I do not want to work in the garden but I always keep in mind the work Grammi must have put into her flowers. Then I get busy, working from dawn to dusk for several days cleaning out the dead matter and resetting the bulbs or planting seeds. The colorful summer and autumn display more than repays me for my efforts. It is showy even on the foggiest days. I have named the driveway to my home Wildflower Lane.

Next door to me lives my daughter Lisa, also a lobsterwoman of Maine. She grew up as I did loving to be on the <u>Marion P</u> with her grandpa. Now she is licensed and is the skipper of her own boat. She has 500 traps, hauling about 200 a day. During the cold months she works as a helper on an urchin dragger. Some day when Daddy and I no longer work together my security will be working with Lisa in my same position. We watch the seasons and the years go by while we remain products of our environment living off the sea.

Thinking about Lisa's house along the way to my house on Wildflower Lane, reminds me of learning to ride my first bike. The bike was a hand-me-down to Mama when she was a girl. Grampy Smith was a real handyman at fixing bikes. He had fixed it up for Mama and then when I was eight years old, fixed it up for me. Oh what a sorry mess it was, but it was a bicycle and I wanted to ride so badly. Johnny already had Uncle Melzer's hand-me-down. I just wanted to be alongside, riding not running.

Mama's rusty old twenty-four inch bike had two flat tires, a rickety seat, no back fender, a broken chain, no chain guard and only one pedal. But it had such possibilities under Grampy's skilled hands. He sanded and then painted it red with lobster buoy paint. He fixed all the failing parts using substitutions from other outgrown and forgotten bikes in his yard. When it was ready, Daddy picked it up and brought it home to me

"Here you go, Darlin'," Daddy announced as he unloaded MY bike.

I was so thrilled and also scared of climbing up on it. Although I am a tall woman now, I was pretty tiny for an eight year old then.

Daddy said, "Come over here. I'll hold it steady while you climb up. Your feet do reach the pedals. That's good. Now you just hold on to the handlebars and I will too. See, I'm holding the seat too. Let's go!"

He ran along beside me helping me steer and stay vertical.

"Daddy, Daddy!" I shouted in glee and amazement. "I'm riding my bike!"

"Yes, you are!"

We went to the end of the road and on the way back he said, "You're on your own."

He let go saying, "You're doing fine."

About three seconds later I took a big spill "skunning" my knees and elbows.

He came to me, righted the bike and said, "You're doin' dandy; now get back on."

I did and rode and rode all the way to the end of the road and back for the next two years.

For my tenth birthday I wanted a new bike, a Western Flyer that I had seen in the Western Auto store in Machias. It was beautiful! It had white rubber grips on the handlebars with multi-colored streamers coming out. It had a red reflector and a horn that you squeeze like clowns in the circus use. It cost twenty-five dollars! What a gift! I was some proud of that! Didn't I love that bike! Not many cars came out to Great Wass Island so the road to our house was pretty safe. When I outgrew that birthday beauty, I inherited Uncle Melzer's English bike with the brakes on the handlebars. My grampy and my uncle made sure that this girl had a chance to ride with Johnny anytime.

Uncle Melzer, Mama's youngest brother, was seven years older than Johnny. When I was only six years old, he told Mama he wanted to take me to the carnival in Jonesport. That was a big annual event, especially well-attended because there was no movie theater or skating rink in town. The advance notice posters in the grocery store, the hardware store and the Post Office were successful. Everyone who saw them got excited. I couldn't believe Uncle Melzer wanted to take me!

Since the bridge was not built until two years later, we went over on the passenger boat. It was so exciting to see the rides, smell the hot dogs cooking and see children everywhere eating cotton candy or caramel apples. We had both. Then we stepped up to a booth that invited the customer to throw balls at milk bottles to win prizes. It cost twenty five cents to play. Uncle Melzer knocked the pyramid of stacked up bottles all down on his first try! He won a prize and said, "What do you want, Joan? You choose. The prize will be yours."

I chose a little green walking cane. It was just the right length for me to use as we walked around the carnival grounds. Finally it was time to get back to the passenger boat and go home. When we reached the long wharf where the boat docked on Beals Island, maybe I was so tired I dropped my precious little green cane and it went down between the cracks in the wharf. We knew it would float away never to be seen again.

Uncle Melzer said, "Don't worry. We'll go to a carnival again some time and maybe you can get another prize."

I looked up at him with tears in my eyes, sad that my little green walking cane was gone but hopeful that some day maybe I could get another one.

"Thank you, Uncle Melzer," I said. "I had a good time at the carnival."

CHAPTER 10

My childhood was made rich by the love that surrounded me, the adventures that my brother and I had, and pets. Blackie and Ripper, our two big dogs, were our constant companions. They loved to be with us no matter whether we were going lickety-split down a snowy hill on our sleds or swimming in the pound in the summer. I loved all animals, big and small.

We loved to go to Brownie's Island, a favorite nesting place for gulls, for a picnic. Our favorite activity there was hiking around looking for nests, baby gulls and shells. Black Ducks also nested there. When Della and Richard's grandchildren were here we would take our picnic in their boat. We took crates along to bring back baby gulls. We made little pens for them and got bait to feed them. It was so much fun raising gulls and then letting them go when we thought they were big enough. I guess we got them started being unafraid of people and enjoying bait, old and new! In hindsight, this may not have been in the best interest of these poor little gulls.

In my own yard I loved to catch sparrows, a first sign of spring. I would get a crate and cover up the spaces. Then I would prop it up on a lath and put crumbs in it. I attached a string which I would pull to make it fall down over the trapped bird. I'd sit for hours waiting for curious, hungry ones to enter. It was such fun to reach in and gently pick it up. I would take it in to show Mama and then let it go. It felt so good in my hands. I would never hurt a bird or any animal. If I found a dead one I would bury it in my pet cemetery. If I found one wounded I would take it home to fix it up.

Daddy called me Ellie Mae from the Beverly Hillbillies. She was always carrying critters home just like I did. The first mouse I caught, however, was already in my home. It had found a cozy nook in the woodpile in the basement. When I first saw him, I knew he wanted to be my own personal mouse.

I ran upstairs and into the kitchen. "Mama, I found a mouse in the woodpile. I want to keep him for a pet. Do you have anything I can catch him with?"

Mama went straight to the cupboard and lifted out a wide mouthed gallon mayonnaise jar. She also gave me an apple core she had just discarded from the pie she was making.

"Oh, thank you Mama! I hope I can catch him. All I've seen is his little brown face and beady black eyes. He really has long whiskers too!" I carefully carried the jar downstairs and placed it on its side facing the niche where the mouse had peeked at me.

I just sat quietly on the bottom step waiting for him to go for the apple core. It was not a long wait. Then he was mine! He was fluffy brown and about four inches long, not counting his tail. He really bonded with me probably because I kept him supplied with apple seeds and always held him carefully. He took the apple seeds from my fingers ever so gently, never ever biting me.

Sometimes I put apple seeds on top of the piano when I was practicing. Squeaky, who loved to listen to me play, would sit up peeling the seeds, just mesmerized. When I finished he would sometimes run back and forth along the keyboard. He just wanted to be where my fingers were. Was he looking for more seeds or trying to make music?

"Daddy, will you help me make a little house for Squeaky? I want him to sleep in my room." I asked Daddy one afternoon when he was finished for the day.

"Well, I think I can do that. Let's see if that good strong waxed fruit box is still in the cellar. The box will keep Squeaky's floor from getting soggy."

"Daddy, how will we keep him from chewing through the box? He has strong, sharp little teeth."

"You're right. He does. Well, I'm thinking I could use that leftover stovepipe tin to line the box. I'll bend it down over the top edges to make it smooth for you. Mama doesn't need any more bleeding accidents to fix."

When he had completely lined the fruit box, Daddy brought it upstairs to my room. I was playing with Squeaky on my bed. I put him down in his new little house, but he looked so tiny and lonely. The next day I would try to catch some company for him.

Sure enough! The next day I buried a small mayonnaise jar in the ground with pieces of apple in it. I caught two, but kept only one, Whiskers. Bozo was a biter and didn't get along with the others so I had to let him go. Whiskers and Squeaky became playmates but really I just wanted Squeaky, so in a short time I let Whiskers go too.

One day I came home from school and got on my bed to read. Squeaky loved to run through and under my hair and nuzzle my neck. I didn't know how it happened, but I accidentally lay on him and killed him. When he stopped running and nuzzling I sat up to look for him. There was his beautiful little brown furry body as still as a rock. I screamed! I bawled! I cried my eyes out!

Mama came rushing upstairs. "What happened? What's the matter?" she asked in alarm. "Did Squeaky bite you?"

"No, Mama. I accidentally killed him," I sobbed. "Do you have a piece of silk I can line a match box with for a coffin?"

"Well, let's go see what is in my scrap box," she said.

We found a nice piece of lavender silk that I folded to fit into the sliding match box from the kitchen. Then I took him into the living room and put him on the piano so I could play some funeral songs for him.

Mama was in the kitchen listening and crying as I played "That Lonesome Valley."

Afterwards, I took Squeaky out and buried him in my pet cemetery with several gulls, a crow and two rabbits. He would not be alone, but I was. His death was my first real heartbreak.

During this same time in my life I was crazy about horses. Oh, how I wanted a horse. I could imagine myself riding jauntily along the road and galloping as far as the causeway, the passageway from Great Wass and Beals. In my dreams I even saw myself on horseback with no saddle as my big strong horse swam in the cove.

I would watch horse stories on TV and read everything I could get my hands on about horses. A bookmobile, provided by the state of Maine, came to our school once a month. I loved to climb up in there and amble down that narrow aisle looking for animal books, horse stories in particular.

"Oh, Daddy, I wish I could have a horse," I would repeat over and over. Sometimes I would read a special section from a book to show him how wonderful it could and would be for me to have a horse on Great Wass Island.

Generally he would respond, "I'll talk to your mother. We'll see about it."

Mama, although I never heard her, must have always responded, "No, Elmer, it's just too dangerous."

To keep my burning desire in front of Daddy, I used a can of trap nails and a piece of board to make a sign: I WANT A HORSE! What an effort that was for a twelve year old girl! He saw the sign every day, but I guess never could convince Mama. Or maybe under consideration he realized pet mice, dogs and squirrels would fit better into our lives.

One day when I was out in the woods, I saw a mother with her baby squirrels running around the base of a dead tree where they lived. They were so cunnin'! Oh, how I wanted them to keep as pets.

I ran home, found Daddy and exclaimed, "I found a mother squirrel with two babies in the woods. Come on let me show you."

"All right," he said. "Let me finish straightening out this trap line. We're going to add fifty more traps this year."

As soon as he finished we walked back through the woods together. Sure enough, he saw the tree with an upper and lower hole. We saw the mother inside.

"You stay here and guard them. I'm going to go back for a cage to catch them in."

While he was gone the babies came back into view, chasing each other and their own tails. They weren't much bigger than Squeaky and just as cute.

It wasn't long before Daddy came back carrying an old bird cage that Grammi Smith had had for a parakeet.

"Look," Daddy said. "They have an entrance and an exit from their home. You hold the cage with the open door up against the upper hole. They will come runnin' into that cage as soon as I can smoke them out."

He lit an oily rag and held it into the bottom hole and smoked them up and out and right into my cage. "Here they are, Daddy! All three of them!" I really did not want to keep the mother but had to because the babies weren't weaned yet.

As we walked home, Daddy carrying the cage, I knew I would have to get a bigger home for them. I also knew Mama and Daddy would not be able to afford a squirrel cage.

Johnny and I earned one dollar a week for doing chores. Johnny preferred working with

Mama and I loved helping Daddy. As soon as I was big enough he let me get wood. I had sixteen dollars saved and hoped that would pay for a cage. I could hardly wait to get to Buddy Brown's Hardware Store to see if he had anything useable.

The next afternoon I said to Mama, "I'm going over to Jonesport to see if I can find a bigger cage for the squirrels. I'll call you from Grammi's."

I set out for the three and a half mile walk from home to Jonesport. The first two miles are unpaved but so interesting. The hilly road is lined with alders and raspberry bushes. Sometimes I could see rabbits running as I looked into the deep woods. From the causeway over to Beals Island it was another mile on paved road along a tidal flat.

It was hard not to run down there looking for clams since the tide was out. Daddy and I used to harvest five to six bushels there on a good day. He would dig holes about two and one half feet around and one foot deep. He would let me help pull the roller he had made out of lath on which we could carry a peck. Daddy sold them for two dollars a peck. We also caught razor fish there, really razor clams, by putting salt down in their holes and watching for their heads to come up. We had to be fast and have a strong grip to hold on to them.

This day, however, I had one mission! Getting a bigger cage for my pet squirrels. I walked into

Mr. Brown's store and said, "Hi, Mr. Brown, do you have any squirrel cages for sale?"

He asked, "Squirrel cages?"

"Yes," I said. "Daddy helped me catch a squirrel family that I am going to keep as pets. They are in an old parakeet cage right now. It is too small."

"Well, let me see," he pondered. "I may have something out back. You wait right here while I check."

When he left I looked around the store wishing I could take back presents to Mama and Daddy for letting me keep squirrels as pets.

Mr. Brown came back carrying a huge four foot by five foot wire display cage that he used when he sold parakeets.

"Is this what you have in mind?" he asked.

"Oh, that's perfect! It's exactly what I need!" I exclaimed.

As I examined it imagining my little pets scampering around from shelf to floor and back, I said, "I have only sixteen dollars. Is that enough to pay for it?"

Mr. Brown, smiling like Santa Claus said, "Well, that's exactly what it costs."

I was some happy! "Oh thank you Mr. Brown. May I leave it here while I go over to my Grammi's to call Mama to tell her I got it? She will come and pick it up."

"Of course. I'm glad I hadn't disposed of this old holding cage."

It was fun to get the cage home, clean it out and fix it up for the squirrels. I made a bed for them out of a big rolled oats box that I put shredded newspaper in. I fed them carrots, bread, rolled oats, apples and acorns. When the babies started eating well, I let the mama go. "Chunky and "Cutie" were so different. Cutie bit me so I couldn't handle him but Chunky would sit in my hands and eat peanuts. They both ran all over the house but always came back to their cage and little bed at night.

They hid stuff in the back of the piano; Mama found all sorts of things when she pulled it out for spring cleaning. One time Mama saw Chunky carrying the nutcracker. If she hadn't seen him carry it behind the piano, she would never have known what end it made! Oh, how they loved to run through the house! Once when Mama was washing dishes one ran right up on the sink to watch and fell into the dishpan! And once when I was taking a bath, Chunky came in and slipped into the toilet. I fished him out and fluffed him dry with my towel. Once when Mama had to come to pick us up at school, she couldn't find them when it was time to leave. Oh what a mess we found when we got home! Daddy had made a shelf that extended out from the bathtub. He had finished it so nicely. Well, those little buggers liked the looks of it too. They chewed all around the edge. We couldn't get angry because they were so cute. Having and loving pets expanded all of our hearts.

When Chunky and Cutie were almost a year old, Daddy decided to take the family to our church camp to do some repair on a cottage. We couldn't find anyone to care for our animals: two red squirrels, two hamsters and Blackie. We invited Uncle Melzer, who had been staying with us since Grammi died the year before, to join us on the four hour jaunt in our little red Renault sedan. It was very small. We had to get shots for Blackie to cross the border into New Brunswick, Canada, our destination.

Early the morning of our departure, Daddy said, "Now let's see how we are all going to fit into this car. Melzer, you and Johnny and Joan will all be in the back seat."

"What about Chunky and Cutie?" I asked.

"You'll just have to keep them on the floor in their little cage under your legs. We'll put a blanket over the cage and you can rest your legs on top."

Johnny asked, "Where are the hamsters going to ride?"

"Melzer will have them under his legs. I guess Blackie will be between the cages," Daddy explained.

Mama was in the front of the car packing all of our baggage in the trunk. "Elmer, I think we're going to have to put your tool box under my legs.

We can put our cake on top of that. I'd say we are some packed!"

Daddy backed out of the driveway and we were on our way. We showed the border authorities Blackie's shot record. He sat up handsome, proud and silent, like the other four passengers on the floor. As soon as we arrived at the camp, Daddy made a bigger cage out of window screening and two by fours. It stayed on a table in Johnny's room until we left. On the way home we stopped to see friends in Black's Harbor. When I let Chunky and Cutie out, they ran straight for our friend's pantry. They disturbed nothing and were easy to catch.

One day during the following year Daddy said, "How long do you plan to keep your squirrels?"

"Well," I said, "I suppose they would like to be free. How can I do it?"

Daddy said, "I'll make a small hole in the cellar door so they can come and go from their cage. One day they'll want to stay out."

They must have been really drawn back by my strong love for them because they came home to their cozy oatmeal box bed every night. I played with them before they went back into their cage.

One night, in the middle of the night, Mama woke up to a sound over her head. There was a squirrel peeking down as if to ask, "How do we get to Joan's bedroom from here?" They were in the ceiling tiles beneath the floor above.

Mama came to my door and said, "Your little pets are underneath the floor over our bedroom ceiling. Would you go in that room and call to them?"

I did. They came to me and I carried them back down to their cellar cage.

The next morning at breakfast Daddy said, "We are really going to have to keep the squirrels out now because if they get in between the ceiling and the floor above that's where the wires are. They might chew the wires and cause a fire."

I put their cage outside in the cellarway covering it with a canvas. They came back every night for years. Even after I got married and lived in a trailer, a different house, they came back and entered. Finally it was just Chunky who was returning. He chewed on all the cupboards, a real nuisance. I made a bigger cage to keep him inside. Missing the freedom, he lost some of his spirit. I knew I had to relocate him.

The old abandoned Coast Guard station, about one mile away, seemed like a perfect place It was three stories with spacious bedrooms and an oak spiral staircase winding all the way up to the tower. From up there we could see all over the islands and both sides of Beals. Since we loved to play there as kids, I knew Chunky would too. I could just see him scampering up and down the stairs.

So I put him in his little carrying cage to deposit him a mile from home. He found his way back the same day. Going one and a half miles the next day, I left him at Deep Cove. He returned. The next place was to the Backfield on Alley Bay, three and one half miles away. It took him three days but home he came. Uncle Melzer said, "He must have climbed the highest tree to look around from and get his bearings."

Finally I had to take him over to the mainland to Jonesport where the peat bog is. That is where I said, "Good-bye for good this time, Chunky." He just looked at me stoically as I walked away. I really don't know what end he made. All I know is he was my fun-loving pet for five or six years.

CHAPTER 11

Recalling that trip to Beulah Retreat, our church camp on the St. John's River in New Brunswick, Canada, with Chunky and the other pets reminds me of what a wonderful summer vacation that always was. We went the first two weeks in July before the heavy shedder harvest began. We all looked forward to friends from other churches who would join us there.

My best friend, Grace, was a pastor's daughter who was as adventurous as my other summer friend, Junie. Grace, however, was younger and tinier than I. One time she said, "Let's climb up into the top of the octagon tabernacle. It will be fun to walk on the catwalk."

Remembering Junie walking on the attic beams, and feeling protective, I said, "Grace, aren't you afraid we might slip and fall? It would be a long way down!"

She said, "We won't. We'll be careful. Come on. Let's go."

It never took much to convince me of the thrill of trying something new. Up we went. We hadn't been up there very long when the pastors and officers came in for a board meeting. Grace and I looked at each other with wide eyes and tightly closed lips. We lay down on our bellies and had to stay that way, still as mice, for about two hours. We were so bored! As they filed out, Grace and I began to carefully sit up and move our limbs. When we had climbed down, we agreed that wasn't any fun at all.

Another afternoon while the parents were in a meeting, we went down to Lake Galilee, a rather small pond, to catch green jumping frogs. We made quite a picture, I'm sure, out on a tree that had fallen into the water. Grace's mother liked to keep her dressed up like a little doll every day. That day she had on a pretty sun dress and cute Sunday shoes. I usually wore shorts for play. Well, as might be expected, she fell in.

"Mama's gonna' kill me!" she wailed as she emerged completely soaked.

I said, "She probably won't, but we need to get home right now so you can get dry."

We had to walk along the streets of the campground in front of people's cottages with her dripping wet. Thank heavens no parents were around to see us. We hung up her dress to dry and then cleaned her shoes. It was so nice not to be the victim that time.

The campground had a big hotel where lots of adults without families stayed. We had community meals together in the hotel dining room. The chef, whom I called Cook, had a Scottish accent and called me Lassie. He let his grand daughter Marie and me help peel potatoes. I just loved working and listening to him almost sing his stories.

There was a pier into the lake that we could jump off. The water was so warm for swimming and water skiing. Daddy always hauled our boat and skis so we had lots of opportunities at church camp to practice that sport. I was popular because we had the boat.

Actually Daddy and Mama both loved to water ski at Spring River Lake closer to our home. When we were too little to ski, Daddy made a board for us to use. It was three to four feet long and one and one half feet wide. He added cross boards for us to prop our feet against to keep from slipping. We really enjoyed being pulled on that when we were little and then he taught us to ski. The one who wasn't skiing got to play on the big tractor tire inner tube Daddy had gotten at a garage. It was like a raft for us to jump off.

One day as we were all having fun in the lake, a thunderstorm came up. Because the lake was located down in a valley, the loud echoes of the thunder resounded over and over. When the hail started coming, we all rushed to the car for safety.

Daddy said, "When the storm is over we'll have to load everything up to haul home."

Johnny yelled, "Oh, look at that man!"

We all saw a man in just his swim trunks running toward his car with blood streaming down his back. The hail had hit him hard! He really had to get home.

Daddy said, "We're going to have to get some help to haul our trailer out. It's mired in the mud down there."

Although we couldn't ask the hail victim, we did find a few other men plus Johnny and me to push as Mama drove the car up the hill.

We loved living on our island, but we also loved mini-vacations away from home. Actually any time Daddy wasn't hauling provided us with vacation time.

The Fourth of July community picnic offered a vacation type atmosphere on Beals and Great Wass, only about three miles away from our house. All the families went to the Backfield at Alley Bay for a day of feasting and fun. There were refreshments for sale to supplement foods brought by the families. In the morning the games were enjoyed by all ages. Somebody would dig a few holes that would be filled with sawdust. Pennies would be mixed in the sawdust and the youngsters would aggressively begin digging for them. The one who found the most would get a prize. Another game that Mama would not let me participate in was the two-legged race. She imagined my right leg in the burlap bag paired with the left leg of someone twice my size! She saw the potential danger of that! In the warmth of the afternoon the kids would swim in the sun-warmed bay. The fireworks from Pierot's Point in the evening brought a very special day to an end.

There were two other days that occurred too infrequently as I was growing up: a day of flat calm in the spring or early summer for hand-line fishing, and a day for picking "wrinkles". At age eight or nine my hands were too little for gloves but Daddy taught me to fish anyway. It was so exciting when he would start our day by saying, "It looks like a flat calm out there today. Anybody want to go fishing?"

Mama, who got a little seasick in rough waters usually answered "Yes sir, I won't have to take my soda crackers along this time."

Johnny and I would rush out immediately to run over to Della and Richard's cabin. "Della, Richard! Want to go fishin'?" Johnny would call when we were still out on the road.

"You know we do," Della would yell back. "We had just noticed how calm the sea looks today."

"Perfect day for fishin,'" Richard added.

We helped them carry their things over to the wharf where we joined Mama and Daddy already there and busy with getting our gear aboard including the ice to hold our catch. Of course Mama had taken the time to put together a lunch that was one of her specialties. No wonder she spent so much time each day in the kitchen: baking desserts and bread and picking out crabmeat monopolized many of her days.

Daddy ran us out to a lovely spot that he seemed to know would yield the cod and pollock we were after. At that time Daddy could sell the fish, in the round, getting three cents a pound for the cod and one cent for the pollock. Daddy set us up, rigging two or three hooks on a line, insuring a catch of two or three fish at a time.

As everyone seemed to be hauling in more than had been expected, Johnny, always my rival, began to get worked up.

"Daddy, I think Joan has a better place to fish than I do. I'm coming back there." He was up on the bow. I was in the stern. For some reason he threw his line in a mad huff. The wind caught it with the heavy lead sinker and landed the hook right on the top of his hand! It hooked underneath his veins.

"Ow, ow, ow!" he yelled as he looked at his hand. "Ow!"

We all scrambled to see what had happened. Daddy cut the line off the hook and plunged Johnny's hand into cold water in a bucket.

Herman Jr., a friend of ours, fishing alone nearby heard the commotion. "What's going on over there?" he shouted. "Somebody catch a seal?" As he spoke he steered over and came alongside.

"No, Herman." Daddy replied, "Johnny got his hook caught in his hand."

Herman said, "Why don't you let me run Marion and him to shore so they can get to a doctor in Machias?"

"Thank you, Herman, "Daddy said. "There you go, Son. The doctor will fix you up right."

He helped Mama and Johnny board Herman's boat and off they went.

We continued to fish because it was such an excellent day and ended with a catch of about two thousand pounds. Although the flat calm became turbulent aboard, we finished successfully. Mama brought Johnny home with a bandaged hand but a restored spirit.

The other type of one-day vacation continued for many years as Daddy, Mama and I would have a chance to go "wrinkling." Daddy would load several pails for each of us into the motorboat and we would head out to our favorite pool between Fisherman's Island and Crumple Island. We could only get in there when the tide was right, not completely down, and only get out when the tide was nearly up.

"I see my spot comin' up!" Mama shouted from her seat in the bow. There it was, a little rock island with a nice flat ledge for landing Mama and her pails.

"OK, Marion," Daddy said as he steadied the boat for her to disembark. "Joan and I will be right over there. Fill your pails."

"Good luck, Mama!" I said as I eyed our destination.

We pushed on; Daddy moored. Going about our own picking, we did not try to make conversation. We loved watching the big pails fill with periwinkles, those tasty little sea snails in their little conch shells.

Later, thinking about the rising tide, I looked back Mama's way and saw that the tide had come up over the ledge! She was waving her arms wildly in the air.

I yelled, "Oh Daddy, Mama's nearly overflowed! We've got to get her!"

"I'm comin'!" Daddy exclaimed as he grabbed his pails. "Get your pails in the boat, Joan!"

Luckily there was a five- foot high rock that she had climbed up on, lugging her two little pick pails. There she was perched on top like a gull, in her purple sweatshirt, faded denim bib overalls and khaki hip boots with her big pails around her at the base of the rock. Concerned as she was that the tide was going to go over those pails, she kept on picking, right to the top of the rock.

As we pulled in, she said, "Well sir, I was beginning to wonder if you were coming to get me or if I was going to have to swim!"

Our mini vacations, sometimes less than a day long, always refreshed us and tightened the family bonds.

Our first and only big vacation occurred during spring break in 1967. Not wanting to miss services on Sunday, we left on Monday and returned the following Saturday.

Our first day in Augusta included staying in a motel and the circus at the armory, the first one for us.

On the second day we went to stay with friends in Orange, New Jersey, right across the bridge from New York City.

Our plans for day three included the top of the Empire State Building and some shopping in a couple of big stores. As we were jostled along the crowded sidewalks, wanting to gawk up and all around, we had to keep our eyes open to see where we were walking.

A man coming down the sidewalk pushing a rack of clothes was yelling, "Watcha u backa!"

Mama looked at him blankly and said, "What in the world is he saying? Is he speaking English?"

Daddy said, "We just need to stay out of his way. Let's go in the store."

The store, like every other one we went in, really didn't have anything Mama and Daddy wanted to buy. Signs with the prices in big black numbers stood prominently over stacks of gaudy neckties, bright socks and flimsy shirts. Nothing a lobster fisherman would ever wear! Getting back to New Jersey required real effort. Once Daddy stopped to ask directions from a man lounging against a storefront. The man looked at Daddy blankly; he didn't speak English. Back in New Jersey that night though, we enjoyed a barbershop quartet concert with our friends.

On the fourth day we drove down to Washington, DC staying in Arlington , VA. Our tour of the White House included the Red Room and the Green Room. I was so excited to be in the house where our president lived! Although everything was roped off, we could see it all. We also visited the Lincoln Memorial, the Jefferson Memorial and finally the Washington Monument, where we took the elevator to the top. Mama put her pocketbook down as if she were in our church on Beals Island, Maine. Filled with all her stuff and all the money for our trip, she didn't want to try to hold it while taking pictures.

She said, "Watch my pocketbook, Joan. I'm going to try to take some good pictures from up here."

"OK," I replied. But that was it; I walked off, trying to see DC from every direction.

When it was time to go back down, Johnny said, "Joan and I want to walk down. Let's not take the elevator."

Oh, how our parents wanted to ride. They were both tired from the sightseeing of the day.

"Come on. Let's walk down." Johnny begged.

Knowing it would nearly ruin them, they gave in. Part way down Mama remembered her purse. Daddy went back up. There it was, right where she had put it down. Daddy's faith in humanity had surely been strengthened. However, when we got to the car, we discovered it had been broken into. Daddy's binoculars and my ten- dollar camera had been taken. We were tired from our big day of sightseeing; Mama and Daddy ached all over. Daddy's heart ached for the thief who had probably never done one day of hard work in his life.

We were almost too tired on day five to tour the Smithsonian, but we did see history on display from the dinosaurs to Wilbur Wright's plane. The big vacation required such a sacrifice on Mama and Daddy's part. They gave up a beautiful week in spring and spent so much money to provide us with a connection to history and a world larger and busier than we could have imagined.

I am fifty- three years old and working with and for the greatest man in the world. There is absolutely nothing he wouldn't do for his family. Today there is absolutely nothing I would not do for him. And I am so happy that we all live at Black Duck Cove on Great Wass Island, Maine.

CHAPTER 12

Tonight Mama, Daddy and I are sitting on the shore rocks at the southern tip of Great Wass Island. The western sky is ablaze turning the rippling surface of the sea shades of pink and purple. We are sipping tea after having just enjoyed a supper of Lipton onion soup burgers on the grill. The grill is the outdoor stove for our favorite place in the world, Pond Camp.

"Daddy, how many years do you think our family has enjoyed doing what we are now?" I asked, as I reflected on the energy and the romantic nature of the Beals.

"Well, you know that my grandfather was the first so that was around 1920. We've been watching that sunset for over eighty years. I'm not sure if any of the older ones ever had burgers as good as these!" he smiled.

"Remember the time we called them skunkburgers?" I asked pinching my nose with my thumb and forefinger.

Mama exclaimed, "Oh my, that was some smell and some taste! But we had to eat that meat; it was all we brought down for the meal."

"That was quite a day!" I recalled. "We had been gradually trying to make the camp lodge comfortable and inviting. That was the day of completely replacing the floor. What a project that was."

Daddy said, "My helper, Toddy, and I loaded all the lumber we needed including the joists on that makeshift barge to haul out here behind Johnny's twenty-eight foot boat. We had quite a load."

"Mama, you and I tried to get everything out of the cabin before they landed."

"But we couldn't get the oil stove through the door," she said. "Remember? We had to wait for them to take the door off."

"Yes, that was exactly what we did as soon as we had the wood all stacked up, ready to start."

"It was amazing to watch you put jacks under the existing cabin joists, lifting it right up," Mama recalled.

"And then what a shock we had! There was that skunk family as surprised as we were. It seemed like everything happened at once. Daddy, you and Toddy went right in and grabbed the little ones while Blackie chased and then tangled with the mother. We just couldn't keep skunks as pets!"

"You're right, Darlin'," Daddy said. "We had a big job to do; we had to get right to it."

Mama said, "Poor Blackie. He and everything around him smelled like skunk for a week!"

"But oh, how good and fresh that new floor was. I think about that day nearly every time I sweep it. It still looks so good. You and Toddy could have been builders in your off seasons, Daddy."

"I remember what it was like before the new floor," Mama said, "Dirt seeped right in on the low side."

"How about that time I opened the door under the sink and three little mice ran out? It was so nice to have a new floor covering old holes and tied tightly to the walls on all sides. We were some proud that night. You finished before nightfall," I recalled.

"Speaking of nightfall," Mama said, "We better take these things up to the cabin before it is completely dark."

Mama and I gathered the dishes and things while Daddy carried our two old thermoses.

As Mama and I walked beside each other, she said, "When your Daddy and I first decided to try to use this camp, it had stood abandoned for years. It was just a one room dilapidated shack with a sleeping loft. We had come down on a pretty spring day to look it over, to see if we would want to make it ours, a place in the woods, a wilderness cabin. Well, sir, we walked all around, saw dust and cobwebs everywhere, no walls, open shelves, 'Yes, let's do it!' we agreed.

"That following week when we were at home I went into town to get cardboard boxes to flatten out to use between the beams for the ceiling and walls. I also got a new set of dishes and began a little stock of cooking items and canned foods. We were really loaded the next time we came down. We piled everything outside until I could scrub the whole place. Just getting it clean made it so inviting. It was like one of your playhouses, Joan. We put up our cardboard ceilings and walls and painted it all white. I put the foods on the small shelf and my new dishes on the larger one. We took the mattress that had been on the loft floor for years out to beat and sun. It was a pretty nice mattress, just in need of fresh air and sunshine. Your Daddy and I had one good sleep that night!"

Daddy had been walking along behind us but got close enough to hear about the good night's sleep. He joined us saying, "Marion, dear, you do remember your starvation diet the next time we came to camp, don't you?"

"Oh, yes! It was late the next spring. You dropped me with some new supplies very early on your way to go out hauling. I was planning to spend the day installing and arranging the new things we had brought down. I remember wanting to be down on the rocks for sunrise and taking my tea down there. I stayed until the sun was bright and warm. When I finally went up to get to work, I actually heard hornets before I saw them. The sun had warmed up the cabin so wherever they were sleeping, they came into the room – swarming! I cautiously peeked in the window and saw what looked like fifty or more flying around in there! I turned and ran back down to the rocks to wait for your return, Elmer."

"Yes, and when I got back you told me all you had eaten the whole day was the candy bar you had in your shirt pocket."

"We waited until almost nightfall to go back to the cabin. You found their nest up in a roof corner of the loft and while they were all in there asleep, you carefully cut it down and carried it outside to burn. I remember asking you over and over, 'Are you sure you got them all?'"

I joined in then by saying, "It was the next afternoon, on Friday, that my friend Lucy and I were going to come out after school. You were letting me drive the car to the causeway by then. So Lucy and I took the school bus that far and then drove home. We changed out of our school clothes, packed our things and began our hike out. I had never done that before, always going in the boat with you."

Daddy said, "You asked me for directions. You were such a smart girl I never thought you might get lost along the way."

"Well, Daddy, we thought we were following your directions exactly. We started out under the old telegraph wires that we knew would lead to the key post house out on the point. We branched off at Three Falls and went on towards the cape shore and Moosabec Lighthouse. It was near dark."

Mama said, "As it kept getting darker and darker, your daddy said he would take Blackie and go to look for you."

"I was hoping that if I kept calling and Blackie kept sniffing we would finally meet."

"You went on the upper heath and we were wandering on the lower. It was so great to hear your voice in the distance, Daddy!" I recalled.

"Meanwhile, I kept hollering from camp to help guide you back," Mama said.

"It was only six o'clock, but it felt like ten. We were so tired!" I sighed.

"When we left camp we rode back in the motorboat but I've certainly walked out many times since in all seasons."

"Oh, that Lucy," Mama interjected, "It has been a long time since you've seen her. You had such fun together in high school."

"Yes, we did," I agreed. "I guess the best fun we had was that time I played the organ in the cemetery. I was fourteen and since you were letting me drive the car as far as the Flying Place, I could visit Lucy often. I parked and then walked over to her house. We loved just walking around Beals together.

When I arrived at her house that afternoon, she suggested, 'Let's check out the flowers in the cemetery. Probably some of the ones thrown out are still good.'

I agreed. We entered the cemetery and went straight to the back where the faded flowers would be ditched down the bank. As we peered down, I nearly shouted to her even though she was right beside me, 'Look! That's a pump organ! I'm going down there to see if I can play it!'

It worked! I could!

Earlier we had seen a familiar town figure wandering the streets. I'm sure you know who that was! We knew he would have to walk past the cemetery to get to his house.

Lucy said, 'I'll watch for old Jimmy Swinton to come along on his way home. When I whistle, you start playing. I'm going to hide behind that big headstone.'

'OK,' I said as I began to crawl down the bank. As I waited for her signal I decided on which eerie tunes I could play. When she whistled I began really pumping hard. She came running to the top of the bank laughing hysterically.

'Oh, you should have seen him!' she choked. 'He stopped, looked over this way and then ran as fast as he could towards his house.'

We were both hysterical! That was the most fun we ever had, playing a joke on old Jimmy Swinton."

Mama smiled, but then said, "There were several years that you were not around to have fun with Lucy or to come out here."

She was remembering how I married so young, had my baby girl Lisa and then divorced. Then I moved to Bangor, probably trying to make a new life providing for us with a new job I was not even prepared to do. When I met a man there I thought maybe that was my answer to get back to the place I knew, where I was loved. At first I thought he would want to haul with Daddy but that didn't work out, so another divorce was inevitable. Number three also failed so from then on I was single. Then I knew I wanted so much to come back here to Pond Camp.

One day I said, "Oh how I would love to go to camp. I know you both are too busy to go out right now."

Daddy said, "Myrtle would love to go with you."

"Aunt Myrtle?" I always thought of her as so prim and proper, so elegant. "Really?"

Daddy said, "Your Aunt Myrtle would be the perfect camping partner for you."

She was. That spring we went for the first time and I rediscovered why she was my favorite aunt. We loved doing everything together: playing yahtzee in the late afternoon, watching for deer at sunset and hiking with a little picnic down to the shore. We were walking to the brook one morning for water when I heard a noise high in a spruce tree. We looked up and saw that a Black Duck was entangled in the thick branches; he had one foot hung up. I shinnied up the tree, which had no low branches on it, and reached for him. He didn't try to pick at me as I tucked him under my arm to crawl down. He wouldn't let Aunt Myrtle hold him though, as I tried to examine him. I wanted to see if there was anything I could fix. He had a broken leg which I couldn't splint so I had to let him go. We set him free where he could enter the pond. When he did, we knew we would always be able to recognize him in a flotilla: he swam in circles with just one leg for paddling.

"Daddy, do you remember that moose carcass we found out there along the shore? That autumn Aunt Myrtle and I were here playing our afternoon Yahtzee game. She was rolling her dice when all of a sudden she said 'There's a moose!' He was swimming across the pond. Shortly we couldn't see him because it was dark. We went back home the next morning and really didn't think any more about it except that we had seen a moose swimming."

"Yes, poor devil. He must have gotten lost in a fog and just wandered into the pond. He probably got entangled in eel grass, couldn't get back to shore and drowned," Daddy recounted.

"I wish Aunt Myrtle were here right now. It would be fun to hear her tell about our wonderful pre-Christmas trip. She said she would love to be out here in the snow," I exclaimed.

"Yes, she did," Mama added. "She also loved preparing for Christmas. I guess she thought being out here with you would start off the season right for her."

"It did for both of us," I nodded.

Daddy added, "You and I came down the day before to bring your food and kerosene. In fact, I left you, didn't I?"

"Yes, you did," I answered. "I had so much to do before you brought her back the next day. The first thing I did was go out and cut a pretty spruce up in the heath to bring inside. It was almost five feet tall. I put on two strings of lights. Then I wrapped all the little boxes I had to put on the tree. It looked so cute, ready for Aunt Myrtle's arrival."

"It was some cold as Myrtle and I arrived with the supplies she was bringing," Daddy recalled. "I wondered at the time how you two were going to enjoy the winter camping."

"Well, we did. That next morning and every one following I told Auntie to pick a package off the tree. They were all the same size wrapped in Christmas paper.

'Well, look here!' she cried as she unwrapped her gift.

"It was a box of Jiffy apple cinnamon muffin mix. We prepared the mix and baked our muffins in the oven of the oil burning stove while our roasted coffee perked on top. It was a cozy, fragrant way to start our day. Each morning she picked a package which was a different flavor of muffin: date, blueberry, apple or plain corn. We had your jam, Mama, on the corn muffins to make them sweet.

"That second day we got four inches of large, wet flakes of snow. Perfect for building a snowman! We had such fun stacking up those huge balls of snow to make him taller than either of us. We created a face using stones for his eyes and nose. We had a scarf and hat to add for color and then branches for his arms. After we finished Aunt Myrtle went down to the shore. Before she returned I broke a big icicle off the roof eaves and stuck it in front of our snowman. When she came back I said, 'Look, Aunt Myrtle, we've got a real man here.'

"She wanted to laugh and finally did but then she said, 'Maybe you better take it off. You never know who might come around the corner.' Yes, Aunt Myrtle was prim and proper and oh, so precious!

"At the last of our week here the temperature dropped to near zero. We were able to keep warm by keeping the wood stove going. We shut off the bedrooms and slept on the couch near the stove. We set up a small table close by also for our meals and games of Yahtzee.

"When it was time to pack up to go home we hated to see that wonderful pre-Christmas celebration end. We knew we were going to walk home but had not counted on the wonderful snow covering everything. We were able to sit down on "the mountain" and just slide down, holding our backpacks on our laps."

Mama said, "You two looked like snowmen when you arrived at the back door."

"In June when we would come Auntie and I would put our picnic things in the skiff and with her perched in the stern we would row over to Pond Point Bar. We had our crabmeat and tuna sandwiches, chips and candy bars and sodas in our little cooler. We pulled the skiff right up on the bar and then set up our picnic so that we could see Crumple Island.

"I brought along my mini tape player so we could listen to our favorite music while we ate. We both liked the Pan Pipers at that time. We sat and ate watching the lobster boats and sea ducks only fifty feet from us. They would almost sing along to our music. Otherwise it was so quiet we could hear the water slapping the rocks in the warm sun."

"Now Carolyn came with you two sometimes," Daddy reminded us.

"Oh, yes, she loved it here like we all do," I nodded.

"One time the three of us came out in the dory with the motor on it. It was a little choppy. We were almost to Pond Breaker when it began to get rough; the waves were getting bigger. Carolyn got scared so I pulled in to shore and let her off so she could walk the rest of the way. Auntie was in the bow and was completely at ease. She knew you had taught me how to take the waves without getting swamped, Daddy. By then you had made me into a skilled skipper. Carolyn was walking so she could keep her eyes on us and said she was getting more and more scared because all she could see was the top of our heads when we were down in the valleys of the high waves. It took ten to fifteen minutes until we could get into the calm of the pond. Aunt Myrtle wrote a complete entry about our 'adventure on the high seas' in her journal that night."

"Daddy said, "I would enjoy reading what she wrote after the February trip out here."

Mama added, "That was one to remember, wasn't it Joan?"

"Yes, it was. Aunt Myrtle and I still talk about it whenever we are here. That year we had not been out in the winter so by February we were dying to come. It was pretty cold, but we had been here when it was near zero on our pre-Christmas trip. She told Uncle Ferrell what we wanted to do."

"He decided to ride out with us in the <u>Marion P</u>. So did Lisa," Daddy recalled. "It was a blessing they both were there."

"You and Uncle Ferrell carried the gas tank, two cans of fuel, two batteries and the motor down to the wharf. Aunt Myrtle, Lisa and I carried our food and clothes," I said

Daddy added, "We towed the little boat behind because I knew we would have to moor quite a ways out. The tide would not be right for getting any closer."

"I remember insisting that Myrtle put on a third sweater, one of mine," Mama said. "It was a very windy, chilly day."

"She was bundled up like a teddy bear," I smiled. "But she was nice and warm."

"When we moored, Daddy, you got down in the motorboat first. Then Uncle Ferrell helped Aunt Myrtle and me down. When he was handing down our stuff to us, a big sea came and flipped us right over! We went up in the air and then down under!"

"Myrtle and I were thrown out, Joan, but your foot was stuck under the seat and you had to take off your boot to get free," Daddy said. "I came up and Ferrell threw a rope to me."

"When I came up I saw both of you in the water. You were swimming towards us with the line. I swam over to Aunt Myrtle and pulled her to the overturned boat. She was having a hard time swimming in her three soggy sweaters!"

"When we all got back to the <u>Marion P</u> Ferrell helped me up first and then he and I both helped Myrtle," Daddy recalled.

"And I was the last one, treading in that icy water for so long. I didn't think I could hold on a minute longer. I was starting to get hypothermia. Oh, I have never been so cold!" I shivered at that memory.

"Poor dear," Daddy said. "I opened her up and set out for home. I called you, Marion."

"Oh yes, Elmer! You told me to have a hot bath and hot tea ready for your arrival. Joan, you were blue all over. While you were in the tub I used the hair dryer to help thaw that frozen hair."

He added, "When we were all dry and warm, we couldn't stop talking about the miracle. Usually those big breakers come in threes. If two more had swamped us, we would never have been rescued. Several of our beloved ancestors and friends were lost that very way!

"The good Lord was surely taking care of us that day. We lost the boat, the motor, the two batteries and cans of fuel, but He saved our lives. How thankful we are."

"I could hardly believe it, after that, when you said you were ready to pack up and go back," Mama said.

"Daddy, one time you told me that Aunt Myrtle would love to go camping with me. We both wanted to go back that afternoon, so we did and we stayed for five days."

Our reliving that near tragedy at sea at the end of a full day at Pond Camp tired us all. We loved being together in our special place sharing memories.

After Mama and Daddy went to bed, I took a cup of tea and went out to sit under the stars for a while. Reviewing so many stories kept me thinking about my life until after midnight. As I settled into my own bed under one of Mama's quilts I prayed, "Thank you Lord, for the good haul and my lobster store of memories."

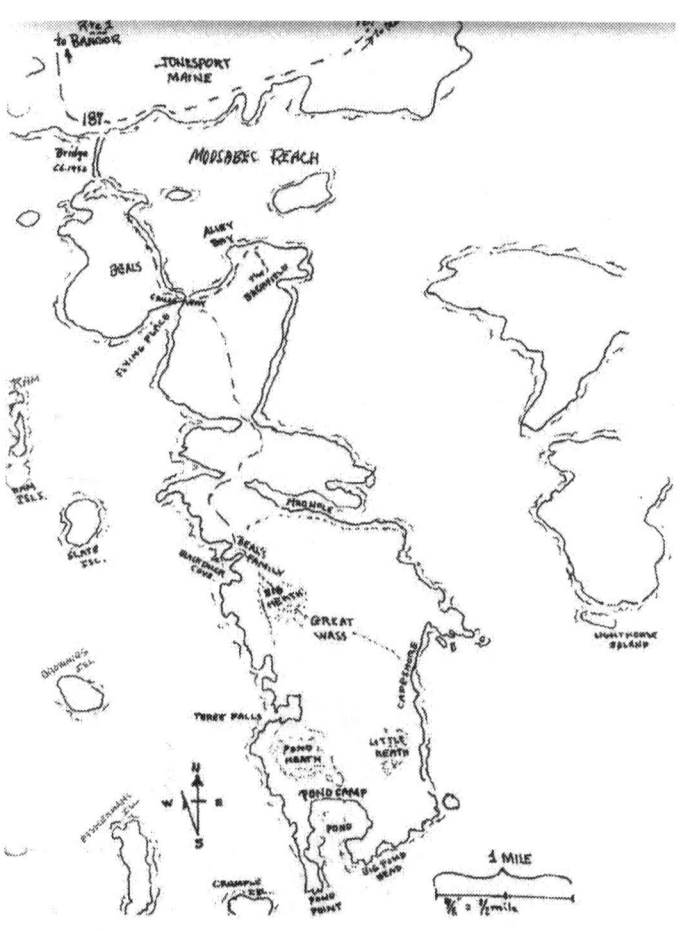

ABOUT THE AUTHOR

Having many stories in my verbal repertoire from my 30 years of teaching English and Spanish, I always felt that someday I might write my first book to memorialize those years. Now that will have to be my second book. This first creation is a result of discovering something and someone entirely new: the lobster industry of Maine and an unusual woman working in that business. She actually prompted the writing by telling me she would love to preserve her childhood memories as a legacy for her daughter. As I listened to her stories on the cassette tapes she sent to me, I imagined my first book could be for a wider audience: people who love lobster, Maine, childhood memories and admirable family values. The thriftiness of content and style are meant to emphasize that characteristic of life in the family.